Let's Walk The Cleveland Way

OTHER WALKING BOOKS BY THE AUTHOR

HER MASTER'S WALKS SERIES:

THE CLEVELAND HILLS

THE HAMBLETON HILLS

THE HOWARDIAN HILLS

SWALEDALE

SWALEDALE A SECOND GLANCE

TEESDALE

WENSLEYDALE

WHARFEDALE

Let's Walk The Cleveland Way

Stephen I. Robinson

BARLEY · PUBLISHING
2018

First published 2018

Barley Publishing
10 Mill Green View
Swarcliffe
Leeds LS14 5JT

www.theclevelandway.co.uk

Copyright © S. I. Robinson 2018

ISBN 978-1-898550-14-3

All rights reserved. No part of this publication
may be reproduced, stored in or introduced into
a retrieval system, or transmitted in any form
by any means, electronic, mechanical, photocopying,
recording or otherwise, without the prior written
permission of the publishers and copyright owners.

Maps © S. I. Robinson
Photographs © S. I. Robinson unless credited otherwise

Maps redrawn from Ordnance Survey mapping and reproduced with
the permission of the Controller of Her Majesty's Stationery Office.
© Crown Copyright - 2016 - OS 100016545.

Printed in Great Britain by:
LGP Print
Century House, Unit 9 Park 2000
Millennium Drive, Leeds LS11 5BP
Telephone 0113 2489262

To Absent Friends

Charm bracelet at Hunt Cliff near Saltburn

Contents

	Acknowledgements	viii
	List of Illustrations	ix
	Preface	xi
	Introduction	1
	Overview	3
	The North York Moors	5
	Helmsley – Ryedale's historic market town	9
Section One	Helmsley to the White Horse	10
	Kilburn – Home of the 'Mouseman'	15
Section Two	The White Horse to Osmotherley	16
	Osmotherley – A welcoming oasis in the hills	23
Section Three	Osmotherley to Clay Bank Top	24
	The Heather Moors – A sea of purple	29
Section Four	Clay Bank Top to Kildale	30
	The Quest for Alum - A Papal Curse	35
Section Five	Kildale to Saltburn-by-the-Sea	36
	The Heritage Coast – Yorkshire's Jurassic Park	42
	Saltburn-by-the-Sea – A Victorian bathing resort	43
Section Six	Saltburn-by-the-Sea to Runswick Bay	44
	Staithes – A prosperous fishing port	49
Section Seven	Runswick Bay to Robin Hood's Bay	50
	Whitby – Shipbuilding and Whaling	57
	Captain James Cook	58
Section Eight	Robin Hood's Bay to Scarborough	60
	Scarborough – Britain's first seaside resort.	67
Section Nine	Scarborough to Filey	68
	Filey – The East Riding of Yorkshire	73
	Places near the Cleveland Way	74
	Equipment – What to take with you	77
	Accommodation and Planning	78
	Lyme disease – Symptoms and Risk Reduction	80
	Bibliography	82
	Addendum	83
	Map key and symbols	84

Acknowledgements

During the preparation of this guide, I received the advice and encouragement of many helpful individuals, without whom this book would probably never have reached fruition.

First and foremost, I would like to express my sincere thanks to David and June Thornton for their editorial advice, proofreading, valuable suggestions and also for correcting my errors. Special thanks to Stephen Spellman, who accompanied me on the trail, for the cover design and his assistance with the inside layout, selection of photographs and many other essential details. I would also like to extend my thanks to Malcolm Hodgson, National Trails Officer for the Cleveland Way, for checking the mapping and directions.

I would also like to express my gratitude to the following organisations for the use of photographs and line drawings: The Lyme Disease Association for their help in preparing the editorial for the pages concerning Lyme disease and for permission to use the drawings and photographs in the article on pages 80-81. The North York Moors National Park Authority image library for permission to use the following photographs: the Bridestones on page 7; Helmsley on page 9; and Heather burning on page 29. The National Maritime Museum, Greenwich, London for permission to use the portrait photograph of Captain James Cook on page 58.

Finally, I would like to thank everyone who replied to my letters and emails regarding the various areas and subjects covered in the book.

Disclaimer

While all reasonable efforts have been made to ensure that the details contained within this guide were correct at the time of publication, neither the author or the publisher can accept any responsibility for errors or omissions, or for changes in the information provided. The author has walked and researched the entire route for the compilation of this guide. However, neither the author nor the publisher can accept any responsibility in connection with any trespass arising from the use of the promoted route or any associated route.

It is the responsibility of all individuals undertaking outdoor pursuits to approach the activity with caution, and if inexperienced, they should do so under appropriate supervision. They should also carry the relevant maps and equipment, wear appropriate clothing and suitable footwear. The pastime described in this book is strenuous, and individuals should ensure that they are suitably fit before attempting to undertake it.

List of Illustrations

Photographs and line drawings

The Cleveland Way from Hundale Point	Cover
Captain Cook Statue, Rievaulx Abbey and Roseberry Topping	Back Cover
Charm Bracelet, Hunt Cliff near Saltburn	vi
Hayburn Wyke	xii
Helmsley Castle	1
The White Horse of Kilburn	5
Young Ralph's Cross	6
The Bridestones – © North York Moors National Park – RJB Photographic	7
Folly of a stone circle, Lord Stones Country Park	8
Helmsley – © North York Moors National Park	9
Rievaulx Abbey	10
The Mouseman Visitor Centre and the mouse trademark	15
Whitestone Cliff, Gormire Lake and Hood Hill	16
The descent into Oakdale	17
Market Cross and Barter Table	23
Mount Grace Priory	24
Gamekeeper burning the heather – © North York Moors National Park	29
The Ingleby Incline	30
Jenny Bradley Cross	32
Site of the Boulby Alum Works	35
Captain Cook's Monument, Easby Moor	36
Roseberry Topping	39
Heritage Coast stone marker	42
Saltburn's Tramway and Pier	43
Railway line along Hunt Cliff, near Saltburn	44
Staithes and Cowbar Nab	49
Old anchor, Runswick Bay	50
Cædmon Cross	51
Whitby Abbey	52
Whalebone Arch, West Cliff	57
Captain James Cook, Nathaniel Dance – © National Maritime Museum, Greenwich, London	58
Captain Cook Statue, West Cliff	59
Robin Hood's Bay	60
Raven Hall Hotel, Ravenscar	61
Castle Hill, Scarborough	67
Scarborough Lighthouse	68
Donkey's taking a break	69
The official end of the Cleveland Way	72
Fisherman Sculpture, Cobble Landing	73
Life cycle of a tick – © Lime Disease Association	80
Erythema migrans rash – © Lime Disease Association	80
Tick removal tools – © Lime Disease Association	81

All Photographs © S. I. Robinson unless credited otherwise above

List of Illustrations cont.

Maps

	Section map showing the route for the Cleveland Way	3
1.	Helmsley to Rievaulx Bridge	12
2.	Rievaulx Bridge to Cold Kirby	13
3.	Cold Kirby to the White Horse	14
4.	The White Horse to Boltby Scar	19
5.	Boltby Scar to Steeple Cross	20
6.	Steeple Cross to Black Hambleton	21
7.	Black Hambleton to Osmotherley	22
8.	Osmotherley to Clain Wood	26
9.	Clain Wood to Carlton Bank	27
10.	Carlton Bank to Clay Bank Top	28
11.	Clay Bank Top to Cockayne Head	32
12.	Cockayne Head to Battersby Crag	33
13.	Battersby Crag to Kildale	34
14.	Kildale to Highcliff Nab	38
15.	Highcliff Nab to Cripple Hill	40
16.	Cripple Hill to Saltburn-by-the-Sea	41
17.	Saltburn-by-the-Sea to Skinningrove	46
18.	Skinningrove to Boulby	47
19.	Boulby to Runswick Bay	48
20.	Runswick Bay to Deepgrove Wyke	53
21.	Deepgrove Wyke to Whitby West Cliff	54
22.	Whitby West Cliff to Widdy Head	55
23.	Widdy Head to Robin Hood's Bay	56
24.	Robin Hood's Bay to Ravenscar	63
25.	Ravenscar to Herbert Hole	64
26.	Herbert Hole to Crook Ness	65
27.	Crook Ness to Scarborough	66
28.	Scarborough to Cayton Bay	70
29.	Cayton Bay to Newbiggin Cliff	71
30.	Newbiggin Cliff to Filey Bus Station	72
	Map showing Youth Hostels and Tourist Information Centres	79
	Temporary Diversion at Hayburn Wyke.	83
	Map Key and Symbols	84

Mileage and Elevation Profiles

Section One	Helmsley to the White Horse	11
Section Two	The White Horse to Osmotherley	18
Section Three	Osmotherley to Clay Bank Top	25
Section Four	Clay Bank Top to Kildale	31
Section Five	Kildale to Saltburn	37
Section Six	Saltburn to Runswick Bay	45
Section Seven	Runswick Bay to Robin Hood's Bay	52
Section Eight	Robin Hood's Bay to Scarborough	62
Section Nine	Scarborough to Filey	69

All maps and profiles © S. I. Robinson

Preface

Let's Walk the Cleveland Way! Well, why not? Although I had completed most of the trail in circular walks, I had never undertaken the route as a long-distance path. To rectify this oversight, I reviewed some of the guidebooks for the trail. However, the maps which they contained were often just highlighted copies from the Ordnance Survey, and in my opinion, the directions given were a little misleading; therefore I decided to write this guide.

After several months of cartography and planning, I was finally ready to begin my journey of discovery and enlightenment. However, as I needed to check the mapping and write notes for the directions and points of interest, my progress along the trail was slower than average. But the Cleveland Way is not a route march, and the leisurely pace allowed extra time to savour the magnificent scenery and take photographs. Besides, time spent walking in the countryside is never wasted, it helps to reduce stress and creates a feeling of euphoria allowing the mind to drift along with the miles.

During the preparation of this guide, I walked the entire length of the Cleveland Way twice. The first survey, for which I had allowed two weeks, took thirteen days to complete, this was due to my slower pace while checking the accuracy of the maps. For the second survey, I walked each section individually using circular or linear routes, depending on the transport available. Both of these journeys were equally enjoyable, and they have left abiding memories.

As a National Trail, the Cleveland Way provides the perfect way to explore the North York Moors National Park and some of the nooks and crannies along the Heritage Coast. To fully appreciate the trail you should allow at least ten days; this will enable you to make detours to villages and historic sites off route. However, it's not necessary to complete the trail as one continuous path. Whether you undertake the walk over a series of weekends or complete each stage individually, is a matter of personal choice.

One of the most gratifying aspects of this National Trail is the infinite variety of mesmerising scenery along the route. From its dramatic heather moorland to the stunning coastline of the North Sea, the Cleveland Way has something for everyone to enjoy. To savour this jewel in the North York Moors crown, just put one foot in front of the other and keep going; but, look back occasionally to admire the spectacular scenery behind you.

Stephen I. Robinson
Leeds, 2018

Hayburn Wyke

Helmsley Castle

Introduction

The Cleveland Way is an inspiring long-distance footpath, which passes through the ever-changing landscape of the beautiful North York Moors National Park. Although it may not be the longest of our National Trails, the Cleveland Way probably affords the most variety. Its spectacular scenery ranges from sylvan valleys and wild heather-clad moorland to dramatic coastal cliffs with sheltered bays and glorious sandy beaches.

One of the principal architects of the Cleveland Way was Alec Falconer, a founder member of the Middlesbrough Rambling Club and an ardent campaigner for walkers' rights under his alias of 'The Rambler'. In 1930, after the foundation of the Youth Hostels Association, Alec conceived the idea of a long distance holiday walk around the outskirts of the moors and the Yorkshire coastline, encouraging the building of hostels all along the way. On 24th May 1969, nearly forty years after its conception, the Cleveland Way officially opened to become the second National Trail in England and Wales. Sadly, Alec Falconer passed away the year before, but his son Alan, who also suggested using *Cleveland Way* as the footpath's title, was present at the opening ceremony which took place at the Helmsley Youth Hostel.

The Cleveland Way begins from the historic market town of Helmsley and traverses the wild, isolated moorlands of the Hambleton and Cleveland Hills en route to the North Sea coastline at Saltburn. The trail crosses the beautiful wooded valley of the river Rye, taking in the splendid ruins of Rievaulx Abbey before continuing to the iconic landmark of the White Horse. However, the most well-known place hereabouts is probably Sutton Bank. Each year many thousands of visitors come here to admire the magnificent panorama over the Vales of Mowbray and York, with Lake Gormire, a natural lake located at the foot of the bank, enhancing the composition. James Herriot, Yorkshire's most famous vet, described this as 'the finest view in England'.

Between Sutton Bank and Saltburn, the Cleveland Way crosses some of the highest summits in the North York Moors, rising to 1490 feet (454m) at Urra Moor, the highest point within the National Park. Moreover, the trail embraces the distinctive cone-shaped peak of Roseberry Topping, which may be small in stature, but it has been dubbed the 'Yorkshire Matterhorn'.

The moorland stages offer an incredible sense of solitude, with only the call of the wild birds disturbing the silence and perhaps a few sheep for company. Throughout most of the year, the moors' scenery is bleak and wild, with areas of green pasture dispersed between vast tracts of the dormant heather moorland. However, in late summer when the heather blossoms, a magnificent sea of purple illuminates the landscape, and the moors are alive with fluttering butterflies and moths, damselflies, and the buzzing of honey bees. Local bee-keepers often bring their hives onto the moors; heather nectar produces delicious honey.

At Saltburn, the Cleveland Way heads south along the stunning coastline of the North Yorkshire and Cleveland Heritage Coast, towards its final destination in the picturesque seaside town of Filey.

The coastal sections of the trail form part of the England Coast Path, which will eventually follow the entire coast of England. When completed, it will be the world's longest coastal path with a total distance of around 2795 miles (4498km). Furthermore, the Cleveland Way also constitutes part of the European funded North Sea Trail, which aims to provide a trail around the coastlines of all the countries that border the North Sea. The route will pass through Scotland, England, Netherlands, Germany, Denmark, Sweden and Norway, making a total distance of just under 3107 miles (5000km).

Yorkshire's dramatic coastline, widely known as the Dinosaur Coast, is world famous for its geology and fossil resources. The shoreline is continually changing due to the instability of the sea cliffs and fossils are prolific in the exposed rocks. Discoveries of ammonites are commonplace, although the remains of more substantial land and marine reptiles do turn up occasionally. However, if you want to confront the dinosaurs more personally, visit the Rotunda Museum, the home of 'Scarborough's Lost Dinosaurs'. The exhibition comprises fossilised evidence of dinosaurs, which roamed around the neighbourhood during the Jurassic period.

The Yorkshire coast has an intriguing history, between 1700 and 1850 many of the picturesque fishing villages like Staithes and Robin Hood's Bay were notorious as smuggling ports. Captain Cook, the British navigator and explorer, began his seafaring career at Whitby, and Whitby Abbey provided the setting for Bram Stoker's novel *Dracula*. During the Civil War, Scarborough Castle endured two sieges, and in the opening months of World War I, German battleships shelled the town and castle from the bay. And the Romans were the first to recognise the importance of Filey – long before Billy Butlin!

The Cleveland Way involves many steep ascents and descents which become slippery in wet and icy conditions; therefore extra caution is advisable. Furthermore, much of the coastal path is unfenced, so it's important to keep to the waymarked route for safety. The coastline is also susceptible to landslips which occasionally result in the trail being diverted. If you should encounter a diversion, ALWAYS follow the signs – NEVER 'carry on regardless!'

Both the moorland and coastal stages of the Cleveland Way explore some of the most beautiful landscapes in the country. However, taking time to visit some of the fascinating places a little further off the route, such as Kilburn, Great Ayton or Guisborough, will make your experience even more enjoyable. Furthermore, dawdling on the Cleveland Way is rigorously recommended!

Overview

About the Maps

The above map shows the area of the **North York Moors National Park**, and the red line indicates the route of the Cleveland Way National Trail, which runs **109 miles (175km)** between **Helmsley and Filey**, meandering along the border of the National Park. There are nine individual stages in this guide, and all of them finish in or within easy reach of a village where accommodation or transport is available.

①	Section One	Helmsley to the White Horse	8¾ miles (14.1km).
②	Section Two	The White Horse to Osmotherley	12¾ miles (20.5km).
③	Section Three	Osmotherley to Clay Bank Top	10¾ miles (17.3km).
④	Section Four	Clay Bank Top to Kildale	9½ miles (15.3km).
⑤	Section Five	Kildale to Saltburn-by-the-Sea	14¾ miles (23.7km).
⑥	Section Six	Saltburn-by-the-Sea to Runswick Bay	12 miles (19.3km).
⑦	Section Seven	Runswick Bay to Robin Hood's Bay	15¼ miles (24.5km).
⑧	Section Eight	Robin Hood's Bay to Scarborough	15 miles (24.1km).
⑨	Section Nine	Scarborough to Filey	10 miles (16.1km).

Each of the distances in the above sections is achievable within a day's walking and should be within the capabilities of most walkers. Nevertheless, it is possible to adjust the daily mileage to suit personal requirements, although the availability of accommodation and transport, especially during the moorland stages, prevents total flexibility. Moreover, the moorland sections have fewer opportunities for refreshments without making some lengthy detours. Plan your itinerary carefully, and allow sufficient time to visit the points of interest and villages such as Mount Grace Priory, Great Ayton and Guisborough which lie just off the trail. Although the Cleveland Way is a challenging walk, completion times are irrelevant. Consequently, you could incorporate a few rest days, allowing you to explore more of the hidden gems in the towns and villages en route.

Incidentally, the fastest official completion time for the trail is 19 hours 53 minutes and 38 seconds by Jason Millward in the 2017 Hardmoors 110 Ultramarathon. The race starts in Filey, and competitors have to finish the 110-mile race within 36 hours.

As a National Trail, the Cleveland Way is waymarked throughout its length. Most of the gates, stiles and signposts carry an acorn symbol, which is the official emblem used to mark the routes of all the English and Welsh National Trails. However, do not rely on waymarking alone to follow the Cleveland Way, always carry a map and compass with you and make sure that you know how to use them.

Each of the strip maps in this book has the route marked in red with numbered arrow pointers, resembling traffic lights, the colours indicate:

- 🟢 The starting point of the map in use.
- 🟠 The intermediate points on each map.
- 🔴 The last point on each map, directing to the next one required.
- 🅐 Detours and alternative paths.

The pointers relate to the detailed directions, which also include a grid reference for the starting point of each stage. When used together these features should help to avoid confusion, although common sense and some preliminary map reading experience are always advantageous.

The scale of the strip maps is 1:28160 (2¼ inches to one mile) and their simplified format should enable most people to follow the route with ease. However, from time to time walls, fences and hedges may be removed, stiles and gates re-sited, new forestry established and buildings demolished. Therefore, it is advisable to take the relevant Ordnance Survey maps and a compass with you. These will help to determine landmarks and locate alternative routes where necessary. The Cleveland Way requires three OS maps: OL26 *North York Moors - West;* OL27 *North York Moors - East;* Explorer 301 *Scarborough, Bridlington and Flamborough Head.*

Sometimes it may become necessary to divert the Cleveland Way to carry out maintenance work, or because the route has changed. Should this occur, always follow the diversion signs along the path and do not attempt to continue along the promoted route of this guide.

The Countryside Code

Respect Protect Enjoy

Respect other people
- Consider the local community and other people enjoying the outdoors
- Leave gates and property as you find them and follow paths unless wider access is available

Protect the natural environment
- Leave no trace of your visit and take your litter home
- Keep dogs under effective control

Enjoy the outdoors
- Plan ahead and be prepared
- Follow advice and local signs

The White Horse of Kilburn

The North York Moors

The North York Moors are a precious natural resource that we can all share and enjoy. From vast sweeping heather moors, distinctive dales and wooded valleys to fascinating geology, history and wildlife, the North York Moors is a land of astonishing diversity.

In 1947, the Hobhouse Report founded the principle that 'the heritage of our beautiful countryside should be held in trust for the benefit of the people'. This opinion formed the basis of the National Parks and Access to the Countryside Act, 1949. The following statement is how the Hobhouse Report described the North York Moors before its designation as a National Park in 1952. 'There are few places elsewhere in Britain, which can offer such extensive and remote tracts of wild and unspoilt scenery within such easy reach of populated areas.' Thanks to this forward-thinking, the North York Moors are now secure for future generations to cherish and enjoy.

The park covers an area of 554 square miles (1435 km^2), bounded by the plain of the Tees to the north, the Vale of Pickering to the south, the broader Vales of Mowbray and York to the west, and the rugged coastline of the North Sea to the east.

With more than 1400 miles (2253km) of public rights of way, the North York Moors National Park offers considerable possibilities to walkers. In addition, on Open Access land within the park you are free to explore the moorland and common land as you wish, using paths and tracks which are not public rights of way – and the choices become virtually unlimited.

Besides the beautiful moorland scenery, the North York Moors is also one of the most wooded of our national parks, with about twenty-two per cent of the area covered by woodland. Around one-third of this is broadleaf woodland consisting of oak, ash, birch and rowan. Shrubs such as hazel and hawthorn thrive in the understorey, while the alder often flourishes in the moist areas along rivers and streams. However, the plantation woodlands, established throughout the twentieth century, are the majority shareholders. The extensive coniferous forests of Boltby, Cropton and Dalby provide a valuable income from commercial timber production. Furthermore, they create an essential range of habitats for wildlife and offer excellent opportunities for a variety of outdoor activities including walking, cycling and horse riding.

The North York Moors is legendary for the rich abundance of its flora and fauna. All the usual flowers such as bluebell, primrose, snowdrop, wild garlic, wood anemone and violet are widespread in the woodland areas, along with many varieties of fungi and lichen. Some of the more unusual plants are drooping sedge, giant horsetail, stinking hellebore and spurge laurel. Moreover, deadly nightshade, also known as the death flower, is native to one or two valleys of the Rye.

Young Ralph's Cross

The diversity of natural habitats provides vital nesting and breeding areas for many species of bird. In the spring curlew, golden plover, lapwing, redshank, snipe, wheatear and many other birds share the heather moors with the resident red grouse. Birds of prey include: goshawks which perform a distinctive 'sky dance' during courting; kestrels hovering almost motionless over the moor; and rare honey buzzards, carrying out their curious 'wing-clapping' flight displays. The steeply wooded dales and valleys are the haunts of the chaffinch, dipper, goldcrest, jay, kingfisher, nightjar, redstart, tree creeper – the list is endless!

Both fallow and roe deer have well-established herds in the woodland regions; fox, hare, shrew, stoat and weasel inhabit the fringes; and innumerable rabbits populate the fields and moorland areas. In addition, there are ten species of bat which breed within the park, including the soprano pipistrelle, Natterer's and the common pipistrelle which exists in almost every village.

The underlying geology of the North York Moors belongs to the Jurassic period, which took place between 200 and 145 million years ago. Throughout this period, variations in sea level left behind layers of rock ranging from shale to sandstone and limestone derived from coral. These deposits are visible along the North Yorkshire and Cleveland Heritage Coast, between Saltburn and Scarborough.

Other places to see rock formations from the Jurassic period include the Forge Valley near Scarborough and the Bridestones in Dalby Forest. During the last Ice Age, which ended around 11,000 years ago, ice sheets covered the area. As the ice melted glacial lakes formed and meltwater broke through low points in the landscape, carving deep, steep-sided valleys – the Forge Valley was one of these. The Bridestones are spectacular pillars of sandstone standing on the edge of a deep ravine. The fascinating shapes seen today are the result of erosion by wind, frost

The Pepperpot stone on the Bridestones nature reserve

and rain over many thousands of years. The stones are the remnants of a sandstone 'cap', laid down about 150 million years ago.

Besides these natural riches, the area possesses a wealth of archaeological and historical interest. There are around three thousand Bronze Age burial mounds, also known as round barrows, tumuli and howes, scattered throughout the moors. The park also contains the largest Iron Age hill fort in northern England, Roman fortifications, medieval castles, monasteries and more than thirty named moorland crosses including Fat Betty and Lilla Cross. The latter is one of the oldest Christian monuments in northern England dating from AD 626. However, the best known of these moorland crosses is possibly Young Ralph's Cross, which stands nine feet tall and provided the North York Moors National Park with its iconic logo.

In the nineteenth century, when the railways reached the area, it became much more accessible and allowed the large-scale mining of ironstone, alum and coal to begin. This, in turn, led to the industrial expansion of Middlesbrough and established the Teesside iron and steel industry. Although nature has helped to reduce the scars left behind by this exploitation, there are still many relics from that era which remain exciting to industrial archaeologists.

Today, the North York Moors remain relatively unsullied by modern enterprises, and the towns and villages contain many appealing features. The picturesque village of Hutton-le-Hole, where sheep roam freely on the spacious green above the stream, once had a busy weaving industry, and it is now the home of the Ryedale Folk Museum. However, the most famous village in the National Park is probably Goathland, which provided the location for 'Aidensfield' in the TV series *Heartbeat*. Moreover, the village's heritage railway station appeared as 'Hogsmeade' station in the *Harry Potter* films.

The North York Moors is one of Great Britain's most treasured landscapes, an area where peace and beauty mingle with an inspiring history for everyone to enjoy.

Folly of a stone circle, Lord Stones Country Park

Helmsley

RYEDALE'S HISTORIC MARKET TOWN

Helmsley is a picturesque market town and has many impressive buildings, including four former coaching inns. The square contains an ancient market cross and an imposing memorial to William, the Second Earl of Feversham, who died in the Battle of the Somme in 1916.

Sited about one mile south-west of Helmsley lies Duncombe Park, the family home of the Duncombes whose senior member holds the title Baron Feversham. The house, completed in 1713, occupies an elevated position overlooking Helmsley Castle and the valley of the river Rye. Following the death of the Second Earl, it became a preparatory school for girls. However, in 1986 the present Lord and Lady Feversham decided to return here and turn Duncombe into a family home again. The estate has 450 acres (182ha) of gardens and parklands, most of which holds the designation of a national nature reserve. It also has many ancient trees and a wide variety of wildlife habitats.

Close to the town are the spectacular ruins of Helmsley Castle, surrounded by extensive earthworks which stands on a rocky outcrop above the river Rye. The first fortress on this site was a timber structure built by Walter l'Espec in the early twelfth century. In 1186 work began on converting the castle to stone. Further additions and strengthening took place throughout the Middle Ages, and it became a formidable fortress. Nevertheless, it saw little action until the Civil War which brought about its destruction. In 1644 Sir Jordan Crosland, of Helmsley, defended the castle for the King. The Royalist forces held out against 1000 Parliamentary troops in a three-month siege, before surrendering honourably, due to lack of food. Consequently, Cromwell ordered the dismantling of the castle's defences, rendering it useless in any future conflicts.

Helmsley

Set against the imposing backdrop of the castle is the Helmsley Walled Garden, a five-acre, working kitchen garden established in 1756 to grow fruit, vegetables and flowers for Duncombe Park. The garden's original site was closer to the river Rye. However, after being washed away in the great flood of 1759, the higher ground near the castle became the new garden plot. The addition of glasshouses in the mid-1800s enabled the garden to grow exotic fruits which were not native to England. After being abandoned in 1984, the garden lay derelict until 1994 when volunteers began to restore it back to its original Victorian splendour. The leader of the restoration was Alison Ticehurst, a nurse whose vision was to help disadvantaged people within the community. To this end, the primary charitable aim of the garden is to provide horticultural therapy and a tranquil, healing environment from which anyone can benefit.

Helmsley to the White Horse
SECTION ONE – 8¾ MILES (14.1KM)

Rievaulx Abbey

The opening section of the Cleveland Way begins with a leisurely stroll along the beautiful sylvan valley of the river Rye, climbing gradually to the limestone plateau of the Hambleton Hills, pausing at one of Yorkshire's most famous attractions – the White Horse of Kilburn.

Assuming that you have previously enjoyed the riches of Helmsley, we begin our journey of discovery from the market square. There are some superb views of Helmsley Castle as we leave the town. The route meanders through the woodland, passing the site of the medieval village of Griff, to reach Rievaulx Bridge and a short detour leads to the impressive Rievaulx Abbey.

Founded in 1132, Rievaulx was the first Cistercian abbey in the North of England. Rievaulx's foundation, initiated by St Bernard of Clairvaux, was part of an ambitious plan for the monastic colonisation of northern England and Scotland. Within a few years, Rievaulx became one of the most influential monasteries in England, a place for meditation, learning and culture. In 1136 the Abbey began to establish colonies. The most important of these was Melrose Abbey, which became Scotland's first Cistercian monastery, endowed by King David.

Walter l'Espec, the great Norman lord of Helmsley, provided most of the abbey's land. In addition, he granted to William, the first abbot, and his twelve monks, the present site on the banks of the river Rye together with land above the valley to the north. In all this amounted to some 1000 acres of arable land. Under the third Abbot, St Aelred (1147-1167) there were 140 choir monks and nearly 500 lay brothers in residence, and the abbey owned over 14,000 sheep. However, expensive enlargements and rebuilding during the thirteenth century resulted in the monastery falling into substantial debt. At the time of the abbey's dissolution in 1538, only the abbot and twenty-two monks remained.

Rievaulx Abbey is an architectural masterpiece and one of the most impressive medieval sites in England. Many of the outbuildings are still standing to a consistent height, and almost the whole range is visible at foundation level. The eastern part of the abbey church rises virtually to its original height, its soaring, three-storey arches conveying the magnificence that it once possessed. The building stone was quarried locally and transported to the abbey site on barges along two canals especially dug for the purpose.

From Rievaulx we pass through the richly wooded valleys of Nettledale and Flassendale to Cold Kirby. The lakes beside the track attract a variety of birds, including Canada geese, coots, mallards, moorhens, mute swans, teal and tufted ducks. Apart from its church, Cold Kirby has little to delay our progress. The present building dates from 1841 replacing a much older church with twelfth-century origins. Only the font and the bells from the earlier church survive. After passing through Hambleton, we cross the busy A170 and then follow a clear track through the woodland to Roulston Scar and the White Horse.

Roulston Scar was the site of a massive hill fort dating back to c.400 BC. The fortifications covered an area of 53 acres (21.5ha), defended by a perimeter 1.3 miles (2km) in length – the most extensive Iron Age hill fort in northern England. The defences comprised a trench 6 feet (2m) deep with a box rampart, fronted by a timber palisade up to 13 feet (4m) high, topped with a defended walkway. The fort occupied a dominant position, utilising the natural defences of cliffs and steep valley sides. Furthermore, it overlooked the territory of the Brigantes tribe. Therefore, it is most likely that the Parisi tribe constructed it, as a 'statement of power' to impress, deter and intimidate their neighbours.

The site, which has been the home of the Yorkshire Gliding Club since 1937, sustained damage from anti-aircraft batteries placed around the central area during World War II. Apparently, the hilltop had been fashionable with German gliding enthusiasts in the 1920s and 1930s. Consequently, the military declared Roulston Scar as a possible Nazi invasion site.

The White Horse is one of Yorkshire's best-known landmarks – on a bright day, it is visible from over 30 miles (48km) away. The horse initially measured 314 feet long (96m) by 228 feet (70m) high, although it's present dimensions are 318 feet (97m) long and 220 feet (67m) high. In 1857 John Hodgson, Kilburn's schoolmaster, marked out the outline of the horse and a team of thirty-one villagers cut away the turf and other vegetation to reveal the grey limestone rock underneath. To make the horse stand out, they deposited several tonnes of lime over the surface. The White Horse, often nicknamed 'the old grey mare', requires regular 'grooming' to keep it in prime condition and 220 gallons (1000 litres) of masonry paint!

SECTION ONE – MILEAGE AND ELEVATION

Start: Helmsley, the market square.
Finish: The White Horse of Kilburn.
Section 1 Distance: 8¾ miles (14.1km).
Total Ascent: 1481 feet (451m).

Grid Ref: SE 613 838.
Grid Ref: SE 514 813.
Total Distance: 8¾ miles (14.1km).
Maximum Elevation: 965 feet (295m).

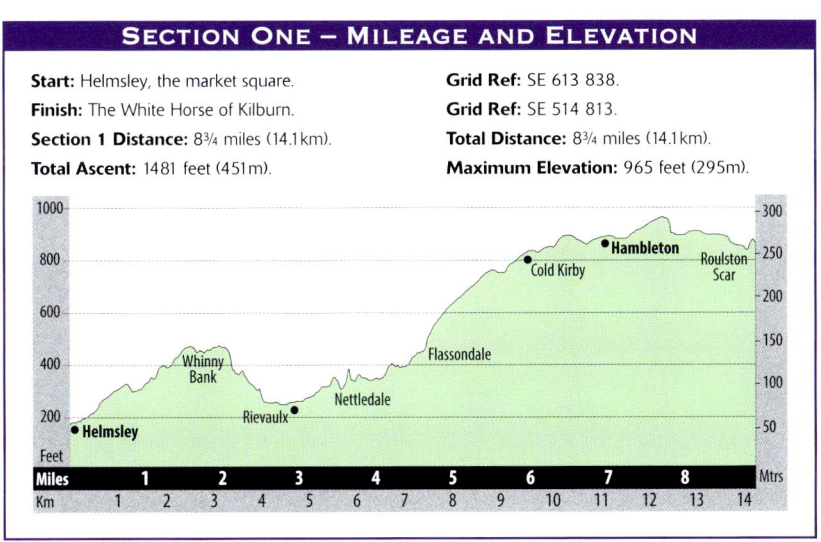

MAP 1
HELMSLEY TO RIEVAULX BRIDGE

1 **613838** Leave the market square by the corner nearest to the church. At the junction turn right into Church Street and follow it to a side street aptly named Cleveland Way.

2 **611839** Turn left *(SP Footpath to Rievaulx)*. At the car park, follow the track to the right, *(SP Cleveland Way - Filey 109 miles)*. A large stone marker seat indicates the official start of the Cleveland Way.

3 **609838** At a fork, continue ahead on a rougher track climbing gradually to a kissing gate *(SP Cleveland Way)*.

4 **607837** Go through the gate and follow the left boundary across two fields.

5 **602836** Pass through a kissing gate on the left *(SP Cleveland Way)* and follow a fenced path to the corner. Turn right *(SP Acorn)* and continue along the fenced path climbing gradually beside the woodland.

6 **596836** Enter the wood to the left *(SP Cleveland Way - Rievaulx Abbey)* and descend some steps to a small clearing. Ascend another flight of steps and follow an enclosed track along the edge of the wood.

7 **591834** Bear left slightly *(SP Cleveland Way)* heading towards Griff Lodge. Pass to the left of the lodge *(SP Cleveland Way)* and follow a good track leading back into the wood, and begin a gradual descent to the road.

8 **580841** Turn left *(SP Cleveland Way - Rievaulx 1m)* and follow the road to Rievaulx Bridge. **CAUTION: busy road!**

9 **574843** Route directions continue from **MAP 2 – POINT 9**.

Refreshments and toilets are available at Rievaulx Abbey.

DETOUR TO RIEVAULX ABBEY

This detour will add an extra 1 mile (1.6km) to the total distance.

A **574843** To visit Rievaulx Abbey, turn right here and follow the road to the abbey. **CAUTION: busy road!** Afterwards, return to Rievaulx Bridge and then follow the route directions from **MAP 2 – POINT 9**.

MAP 2
RIEVAULX BRIDGE TO COLD KIRBY

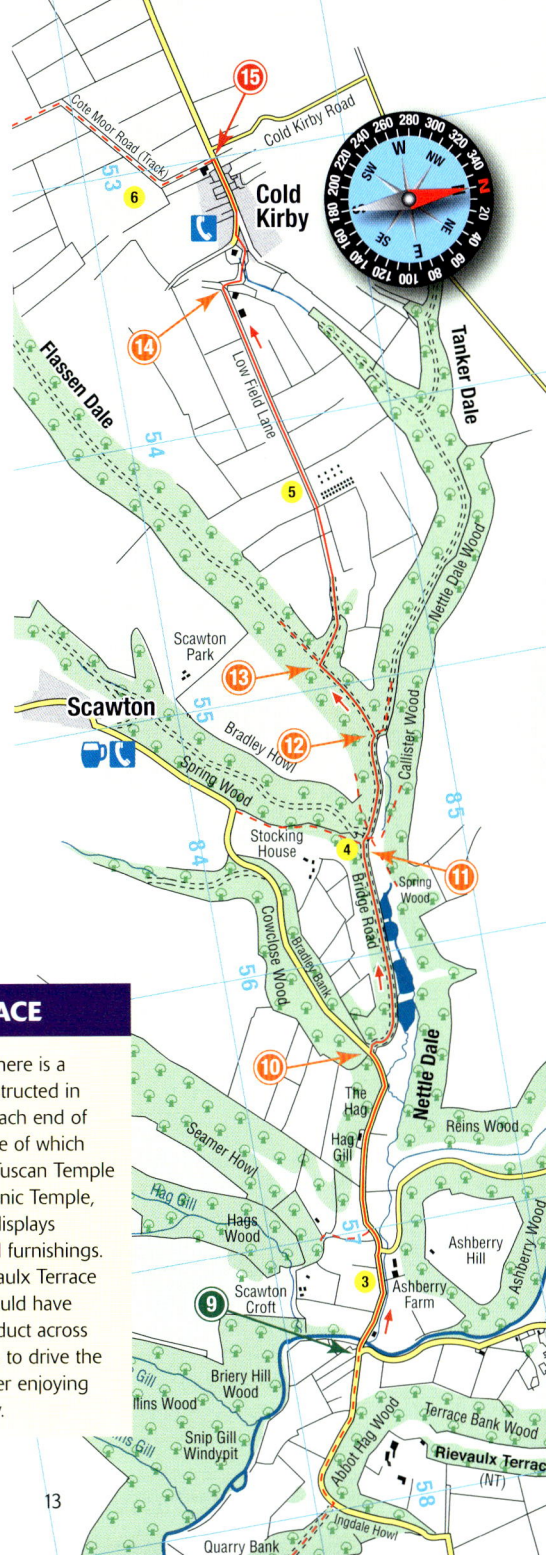

9 **574843** Cross the bridge and follow the road for just over ½ mile (800m) to a sharp left bend. **CAUTION: busy road!**

10 **564845** Leave the road via a forest track on the right *(SP Cleveland Way - Cold Kirby 2m)*. Go through a gate and continue beside some lakes rising gradually to reach a fork.

11 **556846** Take the right fork *(SP Cleveland Way)* and cross the beck via the stepping stones. Go through a gate and climb up to join a broad forest track. Turn left and after a few yards turn right. Follow the track to a junction.

12 **552847** Turn left *(SP Cleveland Way)* and continue along the forest track.

13 **549845** Turn right *(SP Cleveland Way)* and ascend steeply through the wood passing through two gates. After leaving the wood, follow the left boundary through two fields. Continue along an enclosed lane, climbing more gradually to point 14.

14 **535844** Leave the lane via a gap in the right hedge *(SP Cleveland Way)* and descend to the bottom of the dip. Follow the path around to the left and ascend gradually to the road at Cold Kirby. Turn right *(SP Cleveland Way)* and follow the road through the village to Oak House Farm.

15 **530845** Route directions continue from **MAP 3 – POINT 15**.

Refreshments are available at Scawton.

THE RIEVAULX TERRACE

On the hillside above Rievaulx Abbey there is a broad, half-mile long, grass terrace constructed in 1749-57 by Thomas Duncombe II. At each end of the terrace is a classical-style temple, one of which has an exhibition in its basement. The Tuscan Temple is a relatively simple building, but the Ionic Temple, intended for use as a banqueting hall, displays elaborate ceiling paintings and beautiful furnishings. Duncombe's vision was to link the Rievaulx Terrace with Duncombe Park. However, this would have required the construction of a huge viaduct across the valley, enabling Duncombe's guests to drive the three miles from one terrace to the other enjoying spectacular panoramic views all the way.

MAP 3
COLD KIRBY TO THE WHITE HORSE

15 **530845** Leave the village via a gate on the left *(SP Cleveland Way - Sutton Bank 1½m)*, and follow the farm lane.

16 **527840** Turn left, go through a gate and follow the left boundary. Continue through another gate to the woodland edge.

17 **528835** Turn right and follow the track along the forest edge, passing some racing gallops. At the road turn left *(SP Cleveland Way)* and continue to the A170 at Hambleton. **CAUTION: busy road!**

18 **524830** Cross the road, turn right and continue along the road for ¼ mile (400m). At the first junction leave the road via a narrow track *(SP Cleveland Way - White Horse 1m)* and follow it along the Castern Dike.

19 **517826** Turn left *(SP Cleveland Way - White Horse)* and follow a good path around the perimeter of the airfield to the figure of the White Horse.

20 **514813** Route directions continue from **MAP 4 – POINT 1**.

Refreshments are available at Hambleton.

DETOUR TO KILBURN

A **514813** Descend the steps into the car park. Turn right onto the road and follow it down passing the small car park near the bottom of the bank. **CAUTION: busy road!**

B **514805** Continue down to the road junction, turn right and follow the road to Kilburn *(SP Kilburn)*. **CAUTION: busy road!**

C **513796** Return via the outward route to **POINT A**, and then continue using the route directions from **MAP 4 – POINT 1**.

This detour does not constitute part of the Cleveland Way and it will add an extra 2 miles (3.2km) to the total distance. However, you may have decided to make Kilburn your first overnight stop. Whatever the reason – the loss of altitude will have to be regained.

Refreshments and accommodation are available at Kilburn.

Kilburn

HOME OF THE 'MOUSEMAN'

The history of Kilburn is traceable back to the ninth century when Norse invaders began to settle in the valley. Its entry in Domesday Book is 'Chileburne' which translates as Cylla's or Kyle's stream.

The village comprises two individual settlements known as High Kilburn and Low Kilburn, standing about a quarter of a mile apart. High Kilburn rests peacefully on an elevated plateau with its houses arranged around a well-proportioned green. However, the heart of the village is Low Kilburn with the church and the inn standing adjacent to the square. Set into the churchyard wall is the War Memorial. More than forty men from the parish went to fight in the World War I, seven of them were either killed in action or died shortly afterwards as a result of their wounds.

Kilburn's church, dedicated to the Blessed Virgin Mary, is an early Norman structure founded c.1120. The tower dates from 1667 and restoration of the whole church took place in 1869. A sundial on the porch bears the inscription 'Certa Ratio', which when freely translated means 'The right time'. Inside the chapel, there are two coffin stones, dating from the thirteenth century. One bears a pastoral staff and probably represents an abbot of Byland Abbey or a prior of Newburgh Priory; the other one displays a shield with a round boss and the long-shafted martel or fighting hammer of a champion. Kilburn's Champion fought in place of the abbot or prior, in a 'trial by combat', a Norman method used for settling a legal dispute.

The village was the birthplace of Robert Thompson, the 'Mouseman'. His mouse trademark, which he carved on all of his oak furniture, is world-famous. The emblem came about when one of his workmates remarked 'We're all as poor as church mice', after which Robert carved the image of a mouse on the cornice of the church screen that he was working on at the time. Since Robert died in 1955, his business has carried on, and his great-grandsons now run it. The company still uses the mouse for its trademark, or trademarks, as each craftsman carves an individual style of mouse. The Mouseman Visitor Centre tells the story of Mousey Thompson's incredible journey from humble beginnings to furniture legend.

The Mouseman Visitor Centre

Kilburn still holds an annual feast, a four-day event which starts on the Saturday after July 6th. A range of festivities and sports take place, including quoits and a variety of races. The feast comes to an end with the Lord Mayor's procession, when the mock mayor and his mayoress – who is a man dressed in female clothing – tour the village issuing fines to the locals for the daftest offences that they can think up. The landlord of the Forester's Arms suffers an appropriate penalty – a barrel of beer, which everyone can share!

The White Horse to Osmotherley
SECTION TWO – 12¾ MILES (20.5KM)

Whitestone Cliff, Hood Hill and Gormire Lake

Today's journey along the Cleveland Way follows the western edge of the Hambleton Hills overlooking the Vales of York and Mowbray. The reasonably level terrain enables a steady pace, and the scenery is outstanding. However, opportunities for refreshments are limited, so please ensure that you take sufficient snacks and drinks with you.

Resuming our walk from the White Horse, we follow the ridge back along Roulston Scar to Sutton Bank. This ridge is a perfect place to watch for moorland raptors, with buzzards and red kites regularly soaring over the valley searching for prey. The name of the valley separating Roulston Scar and Hood Hill is the Happy Valley, but the distance between them bears the inauspicious title of the Devil's Leap. According to legend the Devil, pursued by the forces of good, leapt from Roulston Scar with a massive boulder adhering to his foot. The Devil carried the stone across the valley setting it down on the ridge of Hood Hill. Apparently the heat from his foot melted a hole in the top of the rock. Incidentally, the stone, which weighs between 16 and 20 tonnes, does have a mark resembling a giant footprint!

As we approach Sutton Bank, there are splendid views of Gormire Lake surrounded by a girdle of trees with the Vale of Mowbray beyond. Sutton Bank is a long, steep hill about 1 mile (1.6km) in length. The hill has been a prominent local landmark since the earliest settlers arrived shortly after the end of the last Ice Age. To accommodate the many people wishing to stop and admire the breathtaking views, the North York Moors National Park opened a new Visitor Centre here in 1997. Together with its 'Window on the Park' exhibition, bookshop and country trails, the centre now welcomes around 130,000 visitors each year.

During the seventeenth and eighteenth centuries, the area between Sutton Bank and Dialstone Farm was famous for horse racing. Furthermore, the Hambleton racecourse was one of England's premier racetracks and revered as 'the Newmarket of the North'. The first races took place here in 1612 when

James I donated a gold cup for the winner of the Royal Plate. Despite the racecourse closing in 1775, the training of racehorses in the area has prevailed, and Hambleton House has been the base for trainer Bryan Smart since 2002.

From Sutton Bank, we continue to Boltby Scar where, once again, the views are impressive. The Hambleton Hills extend to the north and south; and to the west the high fells of the Yorkshire Dales are visible, weather permitting. Below lies Boltby, encircled by rolling green hills. No doubt it was this position which made Boltby Scar the ideal place for an Iron Age hill fort. Until 1961, there was a small D-shaped fort consisting of a five-foot rampart and ditch enclosing three tumuli. In that year the farmer bulldozed it to cultivate the land on which it stood. Nonetheless, a short section of the rampart survives intact, divided by a limestone wall near the edge of the plateau. Fortunately, excavations carried out in 1938 unearthed many ancient artefacts, including some early Bronze Age gold earrings dated c.2200 BC and shards of rimmed jars and bowls from c.1000 BC beneath the rampart. In addition, the interior of the fort produced more of these as well as an urn burial and flint chippings.

Leaving Boltby Scar, we press on to High Barn with its dense thicket of windblown fir trees. Here we descend to Sneck Yate Bank, and then a woodland track leads us onto the narrow lane ascending to High Paradise Farm. Built in the early eighteenth century, High Paradise operated as a dairy farm until the 1980s. Nowadays it functions as a smallholding, and the stables, piggeries and the old corn store presently serve as holiday cottages, and it also has welcoming tearooms.

Near the exit to the farmyard, there is a mosaic depicting a horseshoe. One of twenty-three separate mosaics dotted along a 36 mile (58km) circular trail known as 'The Hambleton Hillside Mosaic Walk' which starts at the Sutton Bank Visitor Centre and offers a variety of inspiring scenery, with cliff tops, woodland and many attractive villages. Local people, both adults and children, created these mosaics to show what makes their area so unique. The designs, inspired by the nearby countryside, include pictures of animals, birds, wildflowers and several represent historical features such as the White Horse of Kilburn.

A short distance from High Paradise our route joins the Hambleton Drove Road, which leads us over Black Hambleton to Oakdale. To the east there are views across the Tabular Hills and prominent in the distance is the Bilsdale television mast. It was erected by the BBC in 1969 to provide coverage to the rural areas of North Yorkshire and Teesside. The mast stands 1234 feet (376m) above sea level and rises to a height of 1032 feet (314.6m), making it one of the highest structures in the United Kingdom.

The descent into Oakdale

The Hambleton Drove Road is an ancient track traversing the plateau of the Hambleton Hills between Swainby and Oldstead. Although opinions differ as to its origin, it was certainly in use long before the Romans arrived and is reputedly one of the oldest roads in England.

According to Dr Frank Elgee, a local archæologist, 'Along this route came long-barrow man as far north as Kepwick Moor, followed by beaker-makers, who were succeeded by the urn folk, whose round barrows mark its course.' Tradition holds that William the Conqueror used this road during his Harrying of the North in 1069. The road had royal protection by 1246, and a record in the *Rievaulx Chartulary* describes it as 'Regalis Via' or the 'King's Way'.

The drove road saw the most activity in the eighteenth century when Scottish drovers used it to bring their cattle to the markets of Malton, York and as far south as London. Herds of between 200 and 300 cattle travelled south along this road from Scotland. The drovers covered distances of 10 to 15 miles (16-24km) each day, and the columns of animals often stretched for over 2 miles (3km). There were regular stopping places along the route, known as stances. These usually had a tavern and essential grazing for the cattle; Limekiln House was one of these stances. The Inn closed in 1890, and it was demolished in 1953 after becoming unsafe. After selling the herd, the drover had to walk back along the drove road carrying the payment to his employer. Moreover, he then had to contend with the constant threat of robbery along the Thieves' Highway – another rather unpromising name for the Hambleton Drove Road.

Black Hambleton marks the northern edge of the Hambleton Hills, and during the descent to Oakdale, we begin our exploration of the Cleveland Hills, and the rocky summit of Roseberry Topping stands out in the distance. Oakdale's reservoirs originally supplied water to Northallerton, but now they offer splendid opportunities for recreation and also encourage a rich variety of wildlife to the area. From Oakdale, we continue to Osmotherley, where good food, a refreshing drink and relaxing bath await!

SECTION TWO – MILEAGE AND ELEVATION

Start: The White Horse of Kilburn.
Finish: Market Cross, Osmotherley.
Section 2 Distance: 12¾ miles (20.5km).
Total Ascent: 1738 feet (530m).

Grid Ref: SE 514 813.
Grid Ref: SE 456 972.
Total Distance: 21½ miles (34.6km).
Maximum Elevation: 1280 feet (390m).

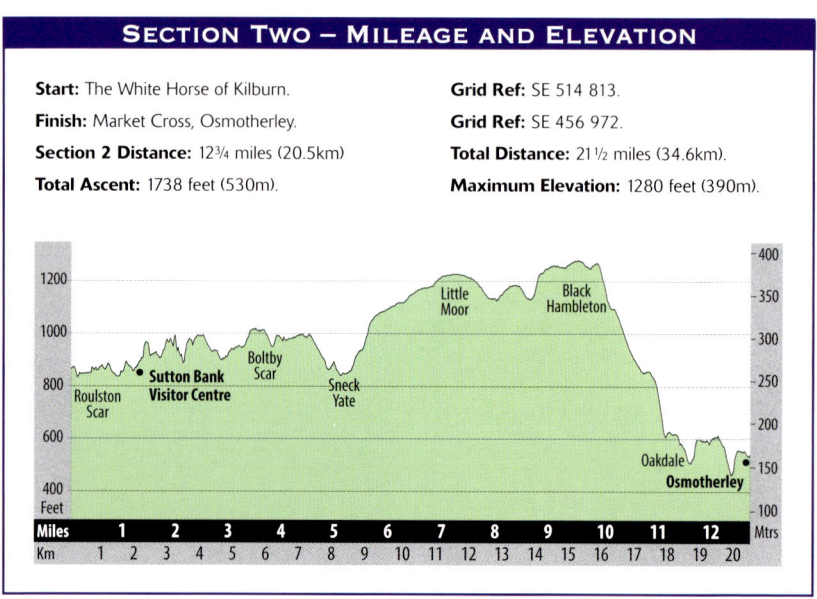

MAP 4
THE WHITE HORSE TO BOLTBY SCAR

① 514813 From the White Horse retrace the outward route along the ridge passing around the perimeter of the airfield, returning to the Castern Dike.

② 517826 Continue straight ahead *(SP Cleveland Way - Sutton Bank)*. When the path forks further on, follow the left fork, which leads to the old viewpoint. Afterwards, follow the path round to the main road.

③ 515830 Cross the A170 road at the top of Sutton Bank. **CAUTION: very busy road!** After a few yards turn left and follow the path to cross the minor road, *(also quite busy)*.

④ 514830 Follow a clear track to a viewpoint platform *(SP Cleveland Way - Sneck Yate 3m)*. Now continue on a clear path to another viewpoint at Whitestone Cliff.

⑤ 507838 Make a short descent from the viewpoint and then take the left fork *(SP Cleveland Way - Sneck Yate)*. Continue on a clear track to Boltby Scar.

⑥ 506856 Route directions continue from **MAP 5 – POINT 6**.

Refreshments and toilets are available at the Sutton Bank Visitor Centre.

GORMIRE LAKE

Gormire is the only natural lake of any real size amidst the moors, a relic of the last Ice Age. The lake formed some 10,000 years ago when a glacial overflow channel became blocked by a landslide of mud and rubble. However, Gormire Lake has no visible feeder streams, and therefore it must rely on underwater springs and rain to maintain its volume; it covers an area of around 6 acres (10.6ha) and is about 27 feet (8m) deep at the centre. Although once thought to have no outlet, the lake does have a small recess on the eastern shore where it overflows and escapes through the rocks. According to one of Gormire's many legends, a duck once penetrated this dark chasm, emerging again to the light of day near Kirkbymoorside, more than 12 miles (19km) away, stripped of all its feathers!

19

MAP 5
BOLTBY SCAR TO STEEPLE CROSS

6 **506856** Continue along the top of Boltby Scar. Go through a gate and follow the wall around to go through another gate.

7 **508863** Keep to the wall side and follow a clear track to High Barn. Take the right fork *(SP Cleveland Way)* and continue over the ridge. Bear left and descend to a gate.

8 **508875** Go through the gate and follow the left track to the road. **CAUTION: busy road!** Cross the road and go through a gate leading into the wood *(SP Cleveland Way Osmotherley 9mls)*. A narrow path leads through the wood, passing through two more gates and leads onto a tarmacked lane.

9 **504883** Bear right *(SP Cleveland Way)* and follow the lane uphill via one gate to High Paradise Farm. Pass to the left of the farm buildings and follow an enclosed track to the Hambleton Drove Road.

10 **505890** Turn left *(SP Cleveland Way)* and follow the track through a gate into Boltby Forest. Continue on a clear path through the wood to a gate at Steeple Cross.

11 **495901** Route directions continue from **MAP 6 – POINT 11**.

Refreshments, accommodation and toilets are available at High Paradise Farm.

THE BEAKER PEOPLE

Near Boltby Scar a limestone fissure, or 'windypit', leads into a series of three small rock chambers. These chambers originally served as winter homes and later as burial pits, for the Bronze Age Beaker People who arrived in Britain c.2300 BC. The Beaker People take their name from the distinctive beakers usually discovered in their burials. The skeletons are normally found in a foetal position, and often the grave includes the remains of arrows, daggers and a single beaker which probably contained a drink for the deceased on their final journey into the afterlife.

WINDYPITS ARE VERY DANGEROUS; PLEASE KEEP WELL CLEAR OF THEM!

MAP 6
STEEPLE CROSS TO BLACK HAMBLETON

11 **495901** Go through the gate and continue on a broad track *(SP The Cleveland Way)*. Follow this track to the site of Limekiln House, marked by a memorial stone.

12 **490919** Continue along the boundary wall, pass through a gate and ascend gradually to White Gill Head

13 **491932** Fork left *(SP Acorn)* and keep close to the boundary wall rising steadily onto Black Hambleton.

14 **481942** Route directions continue from **MAP 7 – POINT 14**.

STEEPLE CROSS

Steeple Cross is one of over thirty named crosses on the North York Moors. In 1290 it was known as Stepingecrosse, which most likely originates from the Old English 'Steapinga' meaning 'dwellers on the slope' or 'cross of the hill-dwellers'. The scant remains of the cross consist of a small piece of the shaft.

Further along the track, there are two boundary stones, carved with 'CT 1770' which refers to Charles Tancred Esq., who was the Lord of the Manor residing at Arden Hall in those days.

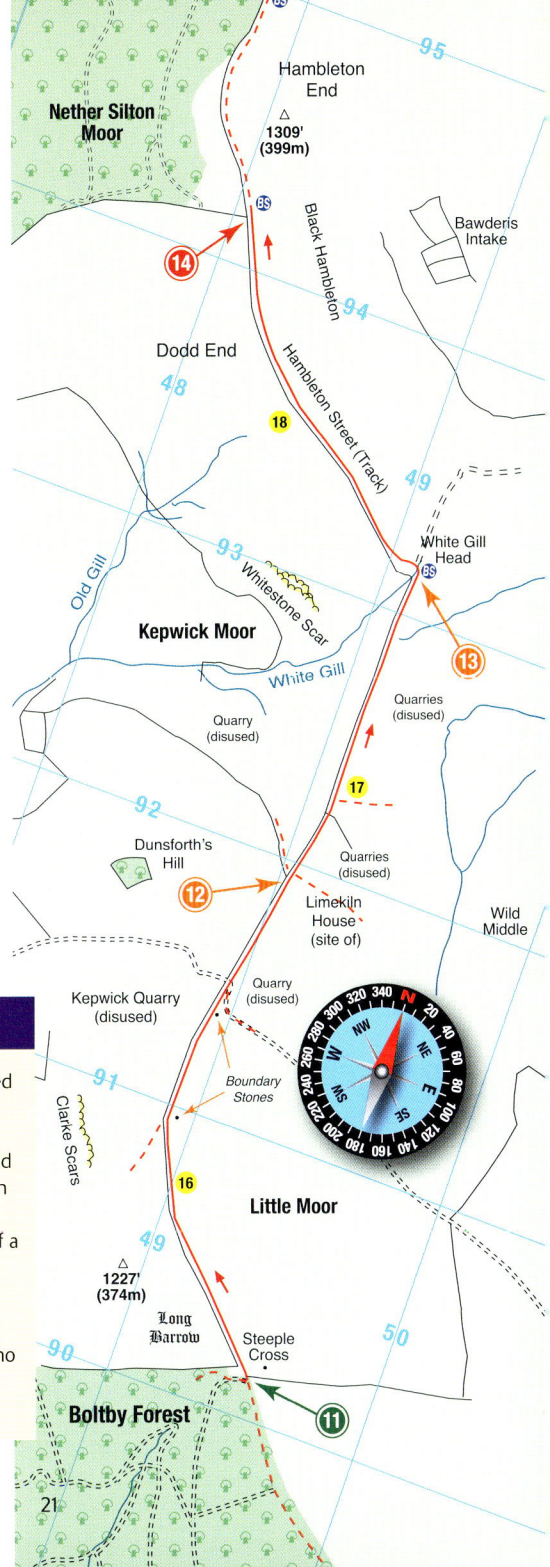

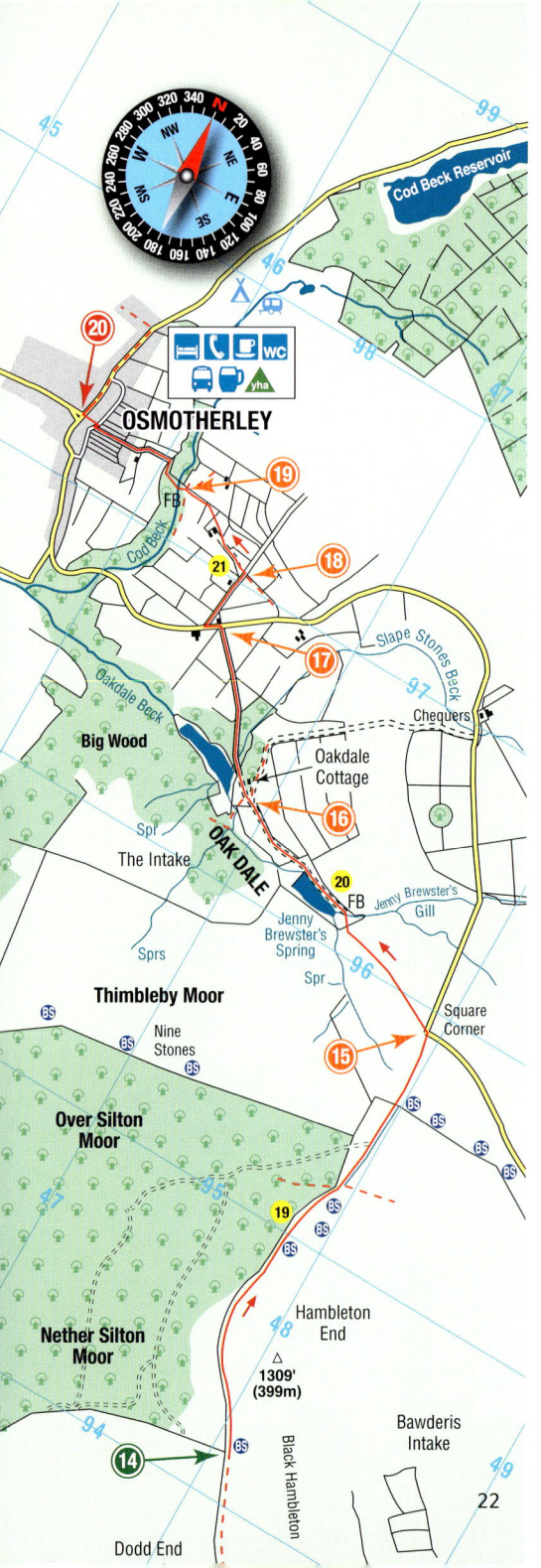

Map 7
Black Hambleton to Osmotherley

14 **481942** Continue beside the boundary wall, pass over the shoulder of Black Hambleton and begin a steady descent. Go through a gate and continue to the road at Square Corner. **CAUTION: busy road!**

15 **479959** Leave the road via a track on the left *(SP Cleveland Way - Osmotherley 2mls)*. Follow a clear path and descend into Oakdale. Cross a footbridge and continue to join a broad track above the reservoir. Go through a gate and remain on the track to Oakdale Cottage.

16 **469963** Descend to the left of the cottage and continue across the bridge. From here an enclosed track leads steeply uphill and returns to the main road. **CAUTION: busy road!**

17 **465968** Turn left *(SP Cleveland Way)* and follow the road downhill for about 50 yards (46m). Turn right *(SP Cleveland Way - Osmotherley)* and follow a rough track uphill to a signpost.

18 **465970** Go through a gap stile on the left *(SP Cleveland Way)*. The path merges with a farm track heading towards White House Farm. Bear right at a signpost *(SP Cleveland Way)* and head to the far right corner of the field. Descend alongside the right boundary via two gates to a footbridge.

19 **461972** Cross the footbridge and follow a fenced path, climbing steeply through the wood. Go through a gate and follow an enclosed track leading onto a back-street at Osmotherley. Cross the street and continue on a path between the cottages which leads into the village centre near the market cross.

20 **456972** Route directions continue from **MAP 8 – POINT 1**.

Refreshments, accommodation and toilets are available at Osmotherley.

Osmotherley

A WELCOMING OASIS IN THE HILLS

Osmotherley or 'Ossy', as it's better known locally, is a picturesque village located on the western fringe of the North York Moors. Its entry in Domesday Book is 'Asmundrelac', which means 'Asmund's clearing'.

According to tradition, the village took its name from an infant Northumbrian prince called Oswy, who tragically drowned after stumbling into a freshwater spring near the summit of Roseberry Topping. The prince's grief-stricken mother died soon afterwards, and her last wish was to rest beside her son. Hence, the name 'Oswy-by-his-mother-lay', subsequently modified to Osmotherley.

The village has had to overcome several setbacks. In 1069, William the Conqueror ravaged the district during his Harrying of the North. Determined to show that he would not tolerate any resistance, William and his army moved north, burning villages, farmsteads and crops, slaughtering the local population. This scorched earth policy meant that most of the area became a depopulated wasteland, a fact which Domesday Book, compiled seventeen years later, confirms. In 1315, marauding Scots ruthlessly sacked the village. Then, in 1348-50, the Black Death afflicted Osmotherley, an event in which almost half the population of the local community succumbed.

At the centre of the village stands the market cross, restored in 1874, although the market, formerly held every Saturday, came to an end in 1823. Beside the cross is a stone barter table, this was a permanent market stall for the sale of dairy produce, mainly butter and cheese. John Wesley, the founder of Methodism, reputedly preached from the barter table during his first visit in 1745. Wesley preached at Osmotherley many times, and one of the first Methodist chapels was established here in 1754.

Market Cross and Barter Table

Just outside the village stands the Shrine of Our Lady of Mount Grace, better known as The Lady Chapel. The chapel received its first licence for the celebration of Mass in 1397, one year before the founding of Mount Grace Priory. The monks probably worshipped here during the building of their monastery at the foot of the hill. Evidently a man named Hugh lived as a hermit in the chapel, although the first mention of a resident priest is 1522 and Catherine of Aragon, first wife of Henry VIII, was one of its benefactors. This historic chapel is worthy of a short detour; it lies just off the trail. If you're staying in the village and still have a little energy left, the chapel is approximately twenty minutes from the market cross.

Two other long distance paths join the Cleveland way near Osmotherley. First, the Coast to Coast Walk on its 192 mile (309km) journey towards Robin Hood's Bay; and then the Lyke Wake Walk, which joins us at Scarth Nick on its 40 mile (64km) trek to Ravenscar.

Osmotherley to Clay Bank Top

SECTION THREE – 10¾ MILES (17.3KM)

Section three is probably the most demanding stage of the Cleveland Way, it traverses the northern ridge of the North York Moors, crossing a series of valleys which drain the moorland pastures. The scenery is invigorating, but there are few places to shelter and the only watering hole en route is Lord Stones Country Park.

The Cleveland Way resumes from the market cross, and within a few minutes, we have two optional detours to consider, one to the Lady Chapel and another to Mount Grace Priory. Both will incur extra time and distance, but if possible they should not be missed

Mount Grace Priory

The priory, founded in 1398 by Thomas de Holand, the nephew of Richard II, bears the illustrious title of 'The House of the Assumption of the Most Blessed Virgin and Saint Nicholas of Mount Grace at Ingleby'. Mount Grace was a Carthusian monastery, whose order observed a strict vow of silence and lived in individual cells where they prayed, studied and slept. Each cell opened into an enclosed garden, and the monks received their meals through a small hatchway in the wall, angled so that they could not see the person who had brought them the meal. Apart from the daily worship in the priory church and silent communal meals on Sundays and feast days, the monks adhered to this hermit-like seclusion. One of the cells has been reconstructed together with a restored herb plot; this helps to provide a glimpse into the lives of the medieval occupants. The history of Mount Grace is uneventful, although it did become a significant centre for the creation of religious texts. Suppression of the priory took place in 1539 when the Second Act of Dissolution forced the prior into surrendering his church to the King's agents.

After a steep climb to Beacon Hill a spectacular panorama unfolds: to the north, the dramatic plateau of the Cleveland Hills; to the east, the high moors of Bilsdale; and the bulk of Black Hambleton dominates the skyline to the south. The scenery remains uplifting as we descend to Scarth Nick. During the last Ice Age, which ended about 11,000 years ago, the ice sheets failed to cover the summits of the North York Moors. Nevertheless, glaciers flowed on either side of the higher land masses and also crept into Scugdale, as the ice melted a glacial lake formed. The lake, about 400 feet (122m) deep and 800 feet (244m) above sea level, overflowed at Scarth Nick cutting a distinct V-shaped valley, a landmark which is visible for many miles to the north.

At Huthwaite Green, the Cleveland Way ascends onto Live Moor and then follows the ridge to the summit of Carlton Moor. Here splendid views extend across the Cleveland Plain to the Eston Hills, Easby Moor and the shapely pinnacle of Roseberry Topping. Following the steep descent to the road, you may wish to take a pit stop at Lord Stones to recharge the batteries!

The next objective is Cringle Moor, which involves a steep ascent to Cringle End where a memorial seat and topograph pay tribute to 'Alec Falconer 1884-1968, Rambler', pause here and enjoy the spectacular views. The topograph will help to identify the distant hills, including Great Shunner Fell in Swaledale, Cross Fell, the highest summit in the Pennines, and even Durham Cathedral is discernible on a brilliant day. At 1427 feet (435m), Cringle Moor is the second highest point on the North York Moors, although the route passes just below the crest there is a narrow track rising through the heather. A cairn sited on the tumulus of Drake Howe marks the summit. The name is a combination of the old English 'draca' – 'dragon' and the old Norse 'haugr' – 'hill or mound' meaning Dragon Hill.

On the col between Cringle Moor and Cold Moor are the remains of Donna Cross. The stone pedestal seen here once held a cross that marked the route from Kirkby in Cleveland to Bilsdale. The initials E and F, carved on the pedestal signify the estate boundary between the Emmerson's of Easby and the Feversham's of Helmsley. From Cold Moor, the route continues across Garfit Gap and ascends steeply to Hasty Bank and the Wainstones.

The Wainstones are a prominent outcrop of hard, sandstone crags overlooking Bilsdale. Their name possibly derives from the Saxon verb 'wánian', meaning to lament or grieve, thus designating them 'the stones of lamentation'. Weathering by wind, rain and ice over many centuries created the striking sculptured pillars and buttresses seen today. 'The Stones', as they are known locally, have been popular with rock climbers for many years, with over 150 routes recorded. The twin pillars of 'the steeple' and 'the needle' are popular climbs.

Leaving Hasty Bank, we descend to the road at Clay Bank Top. A short detour to the left leads to the Clay Bank car park, where a dramatic panorama stretches across the valley to Kildale, with Roseberry Topping and the Cook Monument on Easby Moor as a backdrop.

SECTION THREE – MILEAGE AND ELEVATION

Start: Market Cross, Osmotherley.
Finish: Clay Bank Top.
Section 3 Distance: 10¾ miles (17.3km).
Total Ascent: 2782 feet (847m).

Grid Ref: SE 456 972.
Grid Ref: NZ 573 033.
Total Distance: 32¼ miles (51.9km).
Maximum Elevation: 1371 feet (418m).

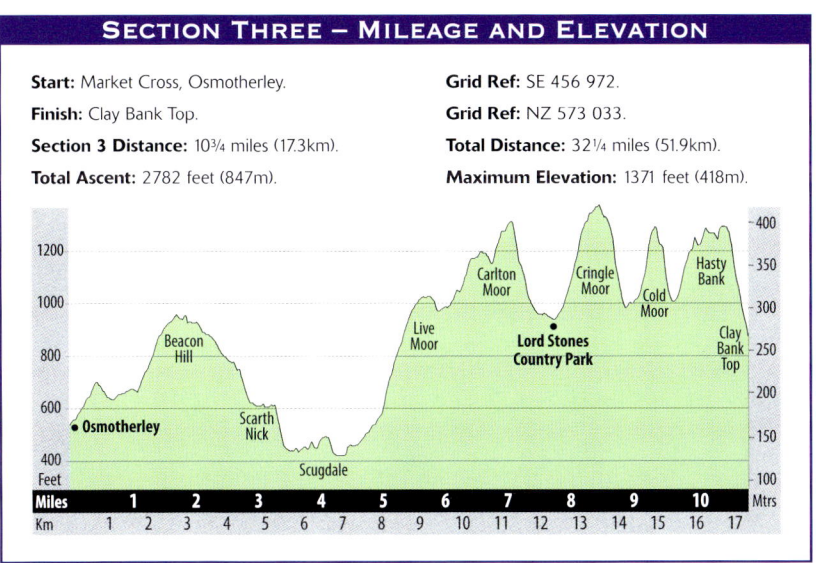

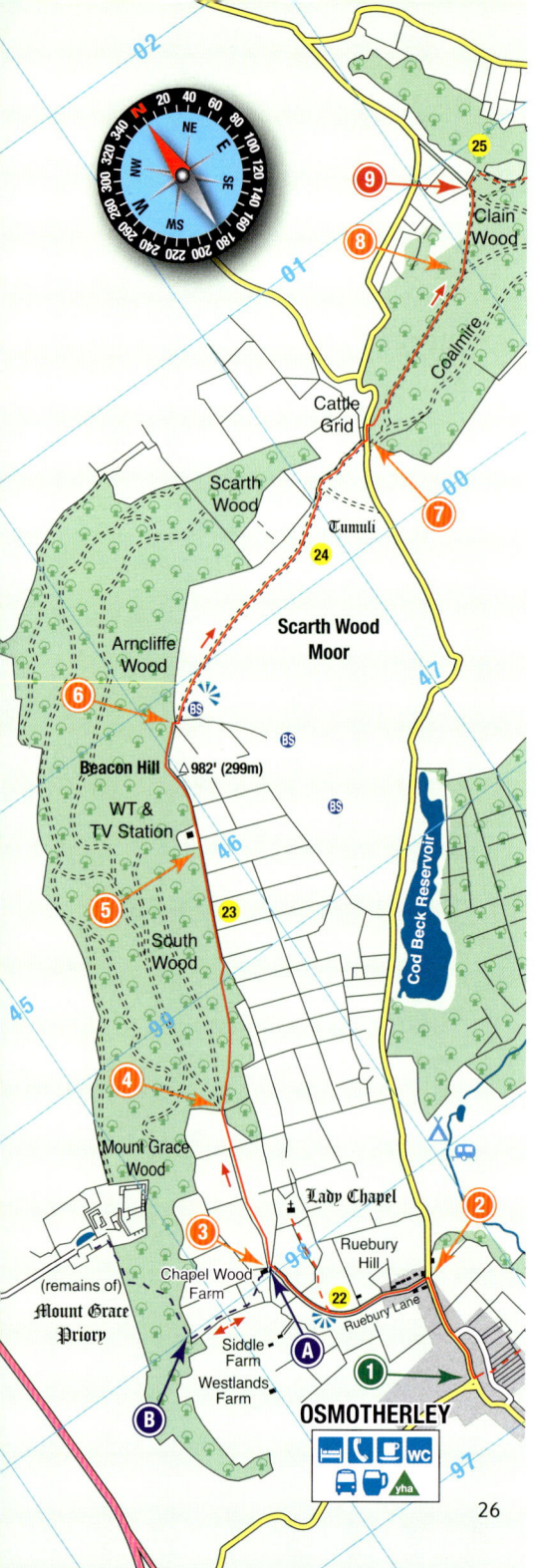

MAP 8
OSMOTHERLEY TO CLAIN WOOD

1 **456972** From the market cross follow the road uphill towards Swainby.

2 **457976** Turn left onto Ruebury Lane *(SP Cleveland Way - Scarth Nick 2½mls)*. Follow the lane to Chapel Wood Farm.

3 **452980** Go through the gate *(SP Cleveland Way)* and follow the left hedge through the field. Continue via two more gates and into South Wood.

4 **454986** A few yards from the gate take the right fork *(SP Cleveland Way)* and begin a steady climb through the wood to a boundary wall. Continue along the wall to the TV signal station.

5 **459995** Continue via two gates passing the TV signal station. Follow the wall round to a boundary gate.

6 **461999** Go through the gate, *(SP Cleveland Way)* turn left and go through another gate. Now follow a clear path descending through the heather. Keep left at a fork and continue down to the road at Scarth Nick. **CAUTION: busy road!**

7 **473003** Turn left and cross the cattle grid. Leave the road via a gate on the right and ascend into the wood *(SP Cleveland Way - Huthwaite Green 1½)*. Turn left onto a forest track *(SP Cleveland Way)* and follow it to a fork.

8 **479006** Bear left, pass the marker stone to Bill Cowley (1915-1994) and descend a steep stepped path. Turn left at the junction and continue towards a gate at the woodland edge.

9 **482009** Route directions continue from **MAP 9 – POINT 9**.

DETOUR TO MOUNT GRACE PRIORY

This detour will add an extra 2 miles (3.2km) to the total distance.

A **452980** Turn left here and descend via three gates into Chapel Wood.

B **448980** Turn right, continue on a clear path leading through two gates to reach the priory. Afterwards, return via outward route and then follow the route directions from **POINT 3 on this map**.

MAP 9
CLAIN WOOD TO CARLTON BANK

9 **482009** Turn right *(SP Cleveland Way)* and follow a clear, undulating path through the wood.

10 **489003** Go through a gate on the left *(SP Cleveland Way)*. Bear right slightly and descend via another gate to cross the beck using the footbridge or the ford. Continue to the road, turn left and follow it uphill to the junction at Huthwaite Green.

11 **493007** Leave the road via a gate to the right of the post box *(SP Cleveland Way - Carlton Bank 2¾)*. Follow a fenced path leading into the wood, go through a gate and ascend along the edge of the wood.

12 **493012** Turn right, go through a gate and follow a stone stepped path climbing steeply through the wood. Go through a gate leading onto the open moor, bear left and follow a paved path climbing steadily to the summit of Live Moor.

13 **505013** Leave the summit and make a relatively short descent before commencing the longer more gradual climb to the OS column at Carlton Bank.

14 **519026** Descend steeply on a narrow paved path leading onto the road near Lord Stones Country Park. **CAUTION: busy road!**

15 **523030** Route directions continue from **MAP 10 – POINT 15**

Refreshments, accommodation and toilets are available at Lords Stones Country Park.

LORD STONES COUNTRY PARK

Since 1990, Lord Stones Cafe has been an oasis to walkers, especially those undertaking the Cleveland Way, the Coast to Coast and other long distance walks. The cafe was refurbished in 2013 and given the grander title of 'Country Park'. Around Lord Stones, there are several Bronze Age burial mounds, including a cairn circle with large protruding stones. The circle measures about 20 feet (6m) across and the site has yielded many finds of flint arrowheads. The estate boundaries of three lords formerly met at these remains, and one surmises that this is where Lord Stones derives its name.

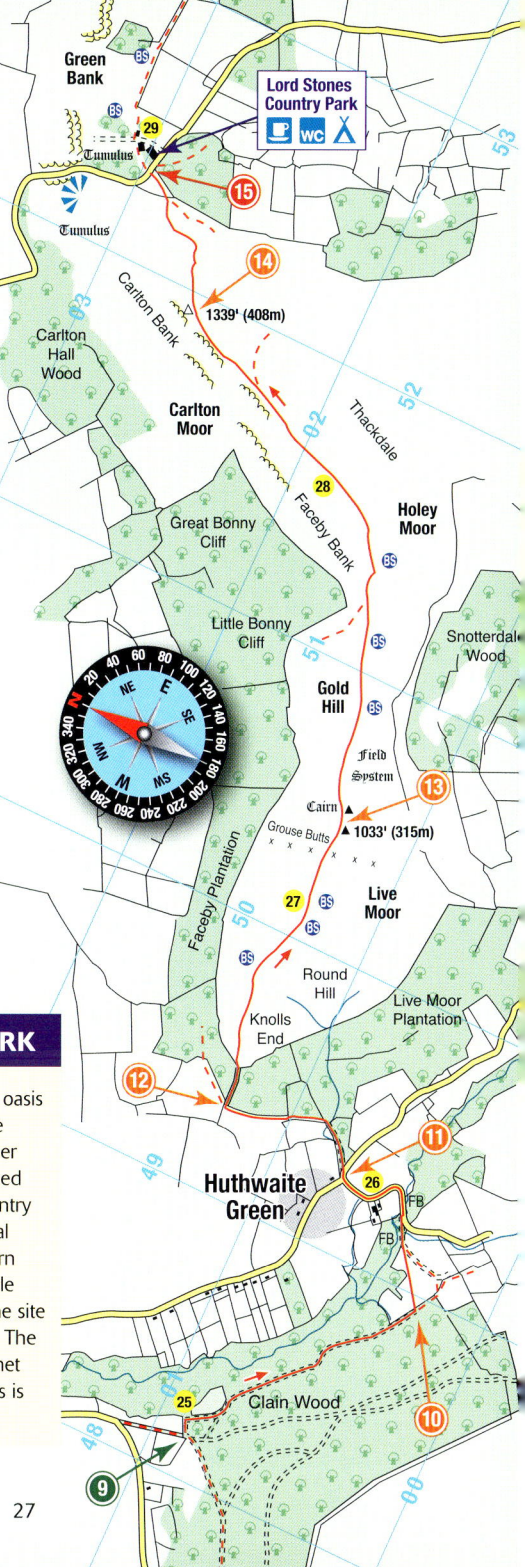

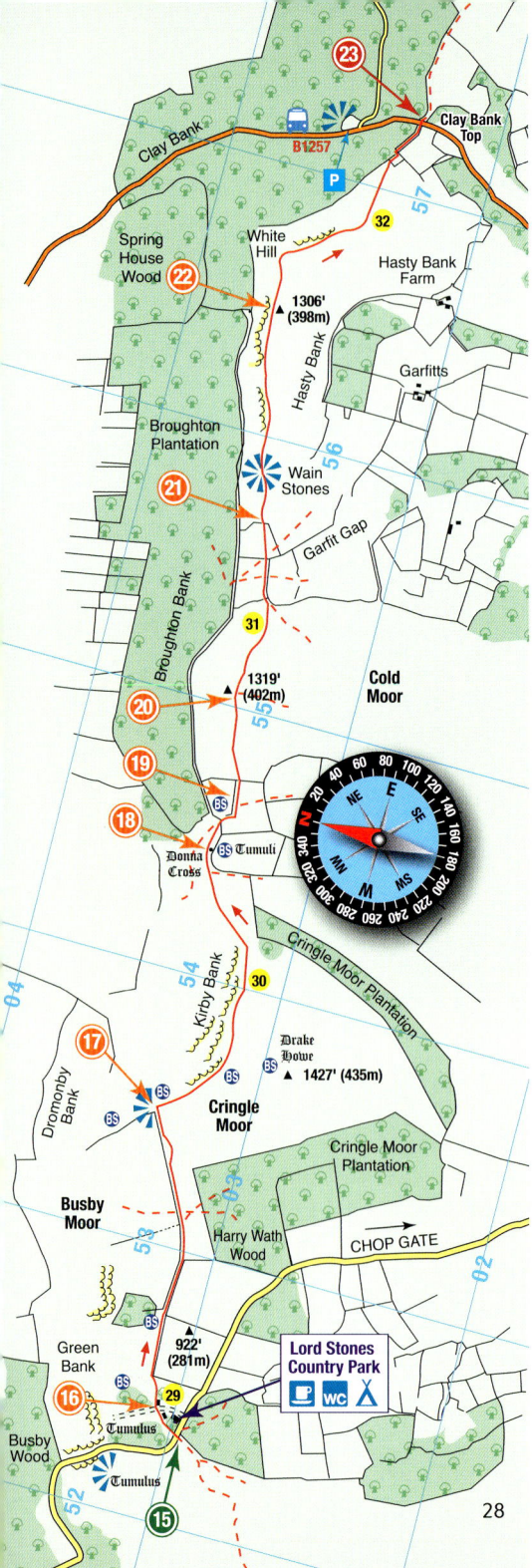

MAP 10
CARLTON BANK TO CLAY BANK TOP

15 **523030** Cross the road and go through the gate opposite *(SP Cleveland Way- Clay Bank 3½ mls)*. Continue on a good track passing behind Lord Stones Country Park and a small copse of trees.

16 **524031** Cross a gravel track and pass a chuck wagon. Bear right and follow the right fence which leads onto an enclosed track. Go through a gate and continue along a paved path which leads steeply uphill to Cringle End.

17 **535034** Continue ascending, after 250 yards (230m) the track becomes paved again. Cross over the shoulder of Drake Howe and then descend steeply down the hillside *(this section is very slippery in wet/icy conditions)*. Bear right and continue to Donna Cross.

18 **545034** Take the right fork *(SP Cleveland Way)* and continue through a gate *(SP Cleveland Way)*. Bear left and follow the left wall to its corner. Turn left and follow the wall to a signpost.

19 **546033** Continue along the wall *(SP Cleveland Way)*, go through a kissing gate and then continue ahead ascending steeply to the summit of Cold Moor.

20 **550034** After crossing the summit descend steeply, go through a gate and continue through two pastures.

21 **557035** Bear left slightly and follow a paved path, climbing steeply to the right of the Wainstones. A scramble across the rocks leads onto another paved path which follows a fairly level track to the summit of Hasty Bank.

22 **565037** From Hasty Bank continue along the paved path over White Hill and then descend steeply to the road at Clay Bank Top *(this section is very slippery in wet/icy conditions)*. **CAUTION: busy road!**

23 **573033** Route directions continue from **MAP 11 – POINT 1**.

Nearest villages to Clay Bank Top offering accommodation and refreshments:

Great Broughton	2¼ miles	(3.6km)
Ingleby Greenhow	2½ miles	(4.0km).
Chop Gate	2¾ miles	(4.4km)

Bus service at Clay Bank Top.

The Heather Moors

A SEA OF PURPLE STRETCHING FOR MILES

Nearly seventy-five per cent of the world's surviving heather moorland is in the UK. Moreover, the North York Moors contain the largest unbroken tract of heather moorland in England and Wales covering roughly one-third of the National Park.

Heather blooms in late summer, transforming the moorland into a sea of purple, extending for many miles in each direction, and the subtle aroma of the heather permeates the air. Every heather flower has thirty seeds; therefore the average heather plant produces up to 150,000 seeds each season. Although heather grows freely and profusely, this wild, dramatic moorland is not a natural environment; it is a managed landscape, created by farmers and landowners who make their living from sheep farming and grouse shooting.

The moorland attracts a great variety of bird species, including curlew, golden plover, lapwing, redshank, short-eared owl and snipe. Around forty pairs of merlin, Britain's smallest bird of prey, reside in the National Park. However, the most common moorland bird is the red grouse, a subspecies of the willow ptarmigan, which is native only to the British Isles and cannot breed in captivity. Consequently, the moors require careful management to allow the grouse to reproduce naturally. Grouse rely on fresh sprigs of heather for food, and the older plants provide them with nesting and shelter. To maintain the balance between young and old plants gamekeepers burn small areas of heather, known as 'swiddens', to encourage new growth.

The burning takes place during the winter and early spring when the ground is wet, and the moor is free from nesting birds. The next year fresh green shoots sprout from underground stems and seeds. By

Gamekeeper burning the heather

burning different patches each year, there are always areas of short heather and tall heather near to each other. Nevertheless, without this management, heather plants would live for around twenty years, and the stems ultimately become very tough and woody, with few leaves or flowers. Furthermore, without grazing by sheep, trees would start to re-appear, and much of this moorland wilderness would slowly revert into woodland.

Sheep also play a significant role in controlling ticks, by acting as 'tick mops'. Dipping the sheep in a pesticide which attracts ticks helps to eliminate many of the harmful parasites before they can move on to infect ground-nesting birds. Using sheep to mop-up ticks in this way also reduces the risk to human visitors from Lyme disease and other debilitating diseases. Don't despair; not all ticks carry the bacteria which causes Lyme disease in humans. However, it's essential to remove all ticks safely and as soon as possible just in case, *(see page 80)*. If you have or think that you have, any symptoms of Lyme disease consult a GP.

Clay Bank Top to Kildale

SECTION FOUR – 9½ MILES (15.3KM)

Between Clay Bank Top and Kildale, we cross the highest part of the North York Moors, and once again the views are magnificent. Although, without a lengthy detour, refreshments are unavailable, so another packed lunch is in order.

From Clay Bank Top a steady climb leads to the broad plateau of Urra Moor. Just off the track is a linear earthwork which traces the western edge of Urra Moor and maintains an almost constant contour, running for about 3 miles (4.8km) across the moor. The origins of this earthwork are uncertain, although it is most likely of Bronze Age construction built to define territorial boundaries and deter attacks from neighbouring tribes.

After the initial ascent, the gradient eases, and the track continues to the summit at Botton Head. However, Round Hill, lying 100 yards (92m) north of the footpath, is the highest point of the North York Moors at 1490 feet (454m). The trig point stands on the Bronze Age burial mound of Botton Howe. Unfortunately, due to the broad summit, bounded in all directions by bleak, windswept moorland, the views are a little disappointing.

The route over the crest passes two intriguing marker stones. First, the 'Hand Stone,' an early eighteenth-century guidepost. Justices at the Sessions, held at Northallerton on 2nd October 1711, issued orders for the erection of guideposts at all crossways throughout the North Riding. Further along the track, we come to the 'Face Stone', so called because it bears the rough carving of a face. Moreover, the 1642 perambulation of the Helmsley estate mentions the Face Stone, describing it as 'the bounder called Faceston'.

From Botton Head, a gradual descent leads to Bloworth Crossing to join the trackbed of the former Rosedale Ironstone

The Ingleby Incline

Railway. Rosedale's railway was an incredible feat of engineering; it linked the ironstone mines in Rosedale to the main railway lines running from Battersby to the iron works in Durham. The line opened in 1861 and trains operated from Battersby to the bottom of the Ingleby Incline – 'Incline Foot'. The empty wagons were removed here and pulled to the top of the incline – 'Incline Top'. Another locomotive took the empty wagons 10½ miles (16.9km) across the moor to Rosedale to collect their cargo. During this crossing, the railway never dropped below an altitude of 1000 feet (305m). The Ingleby Incline was a self-acting incline; it used the weight of ore-laden wagons being lowered down the incline, to raise empty wagons to the moor top. The incline was 4290 feet (1308m) in length, rising from a lower elevation of about 600 feet (183m) to 1370 feet (418m) at the top; the maximum gradient reached was 1 in 5 with an average of 1 in 5.5. Furthermore, there were workers' cottages at both Incline Foot and Incline Top; the occupants nicknamed the latter 'Siberia' because the weather conditions were often very severe on the summit. The Rosedale Ironstone Railway closed in 1929 and little remains of this innovative and industrious period.

At Bloworth Crossing our track parts company with both the Coast to Coast Walk and the Lyke Wake Walk footpaths which continue straight ahead towards their final destinations at Robin Hood's Bay and Ravenscar, respectively. Meanwhile, the Cleveland Way continues over Greenhow Moor, climbing gradually to Burton Howe which stands at 1419 feet (433m).

The tumulus of Burton Howe is a round barrow built during the Early Bronze Age from 2500 to 1500 BC. The barrow has an earth and stone mound standing 6 feet (1.8m) high and 49 feet (15m) in diameter. Excavations in 1956 revealed a turf stack surrounded by a circular kerb. At the centre of this was a stone coffin, containing the cremated remains; other finds include shards of pottery and a clay bead. Moreover, these funerary monuments also served as boundary markers between territorial divisions of land.

Leaving Burton Howe, the route passes another 'Hand Stone', which stands some distance to the right of the track. This one, dated 1757, has three sides carved with hands and directions. In addition, the stone has a hollowed out top covered with a small rock; this is where passers-by could leave alms for poorer travellers. Evidently, this tradition has continued since the stone contained twenty-six pence, five euro cents, and a few other foreign coins on my last visit!

After crossing Battersby Moor, the track descends gradually to the junction with the road to Baysdale, from here the Cleveland Way continues along the road towards Kildale. Baysdale Abbey was one of twelve Cistercian nunneries established in Yorkshire. The Priory of St Mary, first founded at Hutton Rudby c.1162, moved to Baysdale c.1189. At its dissolution in 1539, it housed eleven nuns including the prioress. Nothing remains of the convent, Baysdale Abbey is now a working farm with a few holiday cottages.

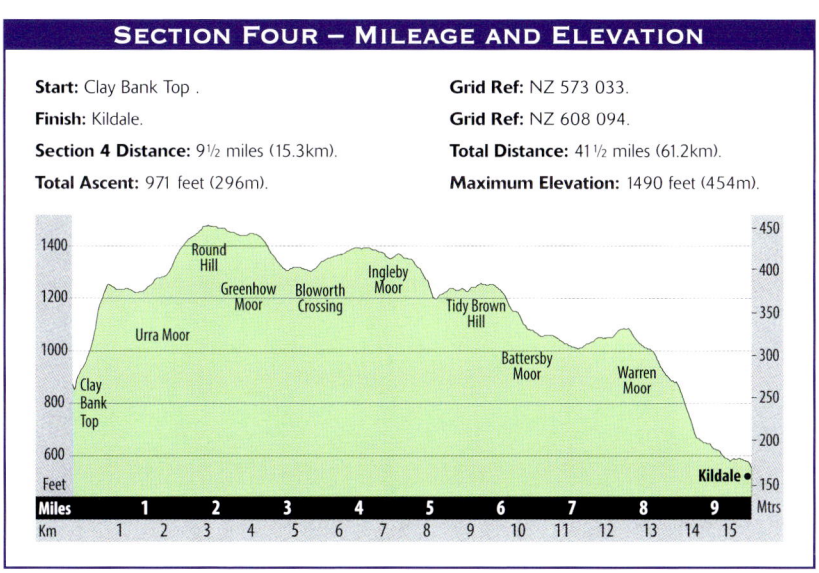

SECTION FOUR – MILEAGE AND ELEVATION

Start: Clay Bank Top .
Finish: Kildale.
Section 4 Distance: 9½ miles (15.3km).
Total Ascent: 971 feet (296m).

Grid Ref: NZ 573 033.
Grid Ref: NZ 608 094.
Total Distance: 41½ miles (61.2km).
Maximum Elevation: 1490 feet (454m).

MAP 11
CLAY BANK TOP TO COCKAYNE HEAD

① **573033** Cross the road and pass through the gate opposite *(SP Cleveland Way - Bloworth Crossing)*. **CAUTION: busy road!** Follow a stone-paved path leading steeply uphill through two gates.

② **579031** Go through a gate leading onto the open moor and follow the paved track to a signpost. Take the left fork *(SP Cleveland Way)* and follow a distinct path across Carr Ridge, ascending more gently between the heather onto Urra Moor.

③ **587019** Bear left, the track becomes broader. Continue climbing to the summit of the track near Round Hill.

④ **594015** The summit of Round Hill stands 100 yards (91m) to the north of the track. Afterwards, return to the main track and continue to a junction of paths at Cockayne Head.

⑤ **603015** Route directions continue from **MAP 12 – POINT 5**.

Jenny Bradley Cross

MAP 12
COCKAYNE HEAD TO BATTERSBY CRAG

5 **603015** Continue straight ahead, pass a line of grouse butts and follow the broad track to a waymark post

6 **610016** Leave the track via a stone-paved path on the right *(Waymark)* and continue through the heather. The path emerges onto another broad stone track. Turn right *(Waymark)* and follow the track for about 300 yards (270m) to a junction of routes and an information point.

7 **616015** Turn left *(SP Cleveland Way)* and follow a broad stony track which ascends gradually across Ingleby Moor. The route passes a pair of standing stones *(the Jenny Bradley Cross)* and continues to the tumulus of Burton Howe.

8 **607032** From Burton Howe, return to the Cleveland Way and continue to a junction of tracks near a green metal gate. The route passes the Hand Stone *(right side of the track)*.

9 **601050** Take the right fork *(SP Cleveland Way)* and continue over Tidy Brown Hill to another junction of tracks.

10 **604061** Route directions continue from **MAP 13 – POINT 10**.

JENNY BRADLEY CROSS

The smaller of the two stones standing beside the track is all that remains of a medieval wayside cross known as Jenny Bradley. The cross survives as a stone plinth and a short section of the shaft. Many moorland crosses have personal names; Bradley may derive from 'broad ley' which means a broad track, but who Jenny was remains a mystery.

The larger stone marks the boundary of the Feversham and Ingleby estates. Inscribed with 'F 1838' for Feversham on the south face and 'SIR W FOWELS' on the north, for Sir William Foulis, the eighth baronet of Ingleby who died in 1845. 'T. A. 1768' may signify the landowners initials and the date of the original boundary agreement.

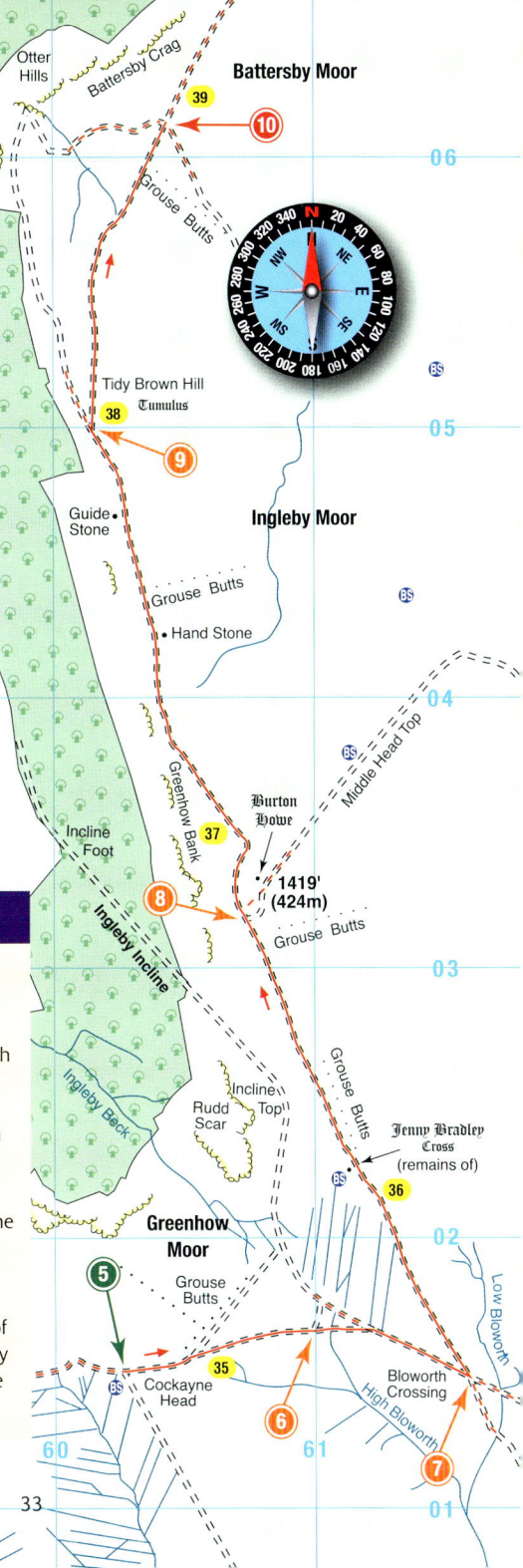

33

MAP 13
BATTERSBY CRAG TO KILDALE

10 **604061** Continue straight ahead across Battersby Moor and ascend through two gates to reach the road junction.

11 **610070** Bear left *(SP Cleveland Way - Kildale 2 miles)* and follow the road uphill to a cattle grid.

12 **616076** Cross the cattle grid and continue along the road. Begin a long descent, which becomes steeper as it passes The Park. Cross another cattle grid and continue to the main road. **CAUTION: busy road!**

13 **604092** Turn right and follow the road for about 300 yards (270m) to the junction at Kildale.

14 **608094** Route directions continue from **MAP 14 – POINT 1.**

Refreshments, limited accommodation and toilets are available at Kildale.

Other villages offering refreshments and accommodation:

Great Ayton 4½ miles (7.2km).

Kildale has a railway station.

KILDALE

The earliest settlement of significance was founded by the Vikings and the name, which means 'narrow valley', is attributed to them. In 1868, during the rebuilding of St Cuthbert's Church, evidence of pagan Viking burials was unearthed. Several skeletons along with swords, daggers, a battleaxe, a whetstone, buckles and other personal items were found under the old floor.

On the small triangular green at the entrance to the village, there is a memorial stone to John Wesley inscribed, 'This stone marks the site of a tree under which John Wesley is said to have preached c.1772'.

The Quest for Alum
A Papal Curse

Site of the Boulby Alum Works

Until the end of the sixteenth century, the secret process for the production of alum was under the strict control of a papal monopoly. At that time, around eighty per cent of Britain's exports were textiles, which relied on the dye fixative obtained from alum.

A succession of British monarchs had long sought the secrets of alum. In 1595 during the reign of Queen Elizabeth I, the North-East textile entrepreneur, Sir Thomas Chaloner was travelling in Italy. While visiting the papal alum quarries at Tofla on the outskirts of Rome, he noticed that the rocks were similar to those on his estates in Guisborough. Based on these observations, Chaloner discerned that he might be able to produce alum on his lands in Yorkshire.

According to one account, Sir Thomas then persuaded some of the papal workers who knew all of the secrets for alum production to return with him to Yorkshire. Supposedly, he concealed them in large barrels and smuggled them out of Italy aboard his ship. However, when Pope Clement VIII learned of this transgression, he excommunicated Chaloner and the workmen; he also issued a terrible curse on them. The curse extended to Chaloner's family, its future ventures and his descendants forever!

Nevertheless, despite the papal curse, Chaloner's alum business became hugely successful and established one of the first large-scale chemical industries in north-east England. The Pope had been exporting alum to England at £52 per ton. But the new supply from the British market cost just £11 per ton. Once the English alum industry had taken root, the Crown, under James I of England, imposed a monopoly of its own and banned all imports from abroad. Moreover, in recognition of his achievement, Sir Thomas received a pension from the King.

When Charles I ascended to the throne in 1625, he confiscated much of the Chaloner's estate because of the alum mined there. The Crown claimed them as royal mines and set up a syndicate for distributing their wealth; an act which angered the Chaloner family by depriving them of the riches that the alum produced. Furthermore, it sowed the seeds of hatred and vengeance, which manifested during the English Civil War and at the trial of the ill-fated King in 1649.

Both Thomas and James Chaloner, the sons of Sir Thomas, served among the 135 commissioners of the court which tried King Charles. Subsequently, Thomas signed the King's death warrant, but James did not. But after the restoration of the monarchy under Charles II in 1660, both brothers had to face charges of regicide and high treason. However, Thomas escaped to the Netherlands, where he died in 1661, James died in July 1660 from an illness contracted in prison. Perhaps both of these events were the result the papal curse?

Kildale to Saltburn-by-the-Sea

SECTION FIVE – 14¾ MILES (23.7KM)

Today we make our way to the coast at Saltburn, visiting Captain Cook's Monument on Easby Moor and Roseberry Topping – 'the Yorkshire Matterhorn'. The trail continues through Guisborough Woods, where we leave the moors behind. At Highcliff Nab there are spectacular views over Guisborough and, on a bright day, the North Sea is visible.

Captain Cook's Monument

From Kildale our route crosses the river Leven and then follows the road to Bankside Farm. The farmhouse building reflects the style of a Danish longhouse. Traditionally, longhouses were built lengthwise down the slope of a hill; they had a living area, out-buildings, cowshed and pigsty in-line. The farmer and his family lived at the higher end of the building; their livestock occupied the lower levels, enabling any slurry to drain away from the dwelling via the end wall. Incidentally, the river Leven is the longest tributary of the river Tees.

Standing atop Easby Moor is Captain Cook's Monument, which rises 51 feet (16m) in height and becomes visible just before we reach the summit. It was erected in 1827 by Robert Campion, a banker from Whitby, to honour Cleveland's most famous mariner and explorer. The panorama from the memorial is inspiring with views south along the curve of the Cleveland Hills, down into Great Ayton, and across to our next objective – Roseberry Topping, with the Tees Estuary and the North Sea beyond.

As we descend from the monument, a plaque beside the path commemorates the crew of an RAF Lockheed Hudson which crashed near here during World War II. The aircraft took off at 4:10 a.m. on 11th February 1940, from Thornaby-on-Tees airfield to search for enemy minesweepers off the Danish coast. Five minutes into the flight, the aircraft crashed, killing three of the four crewmen. Evidently ice had formed on the wings preventing the plane from gaining adequate height to clear the hills. Leading Aircraftman Athol Barker survived with minor injuries, but was later shot down while flying over Germany on 22nd November 1943.

At Gribdale Gate, the Cleveland Way ascends onto Newton Moor where we make a pilgrimage to Roseberry Topping. Standing at 1049 feet (320m) high, it may not be the largest mountain in the country, although many people revere it as the 'Yorkshire Matterhorn' due to its distinctive profile. Furthermore, Alan Hinkes, the first British mountaineer to climb all fourteen of the world's highest mountains, says it's his favourite hill – and he knows a thing or two about dramatic peaks! The unique shape was the result of a rock fall in 1912 when heavy rain weakened old mine workings and caused the west face to collapse. Apparently the hill derives its name from 'Outhenesberg', old Norse for 'Odin's rock or crag', over time the name became corrupted to 'Ouseberry'. The final change occurred, so they say, by the addition of the initial 'R' from the former village name Newton-under-Ouseberry, by alliteration of the 'r' in 'under'. The second element, Topping, comes from the old Norse word 'toppen', which translates to 'hill'.

After returning from the Topping, the route continues over Hutton Moor to Highcliff Wood where we bid farewell to the heather covered moors and begin a 2½ mile (4km) descent to Slapewath. The viewpoint at Highcliff Nab looks out across Guisborough and the Tees Valley towards Redcar and the North Sea coastline.

Although Slapewath is a peaceful hamlet nowadays, substantial evidence of its former industrial heritage surrounds the area. There were forty collieries, pits and ironstone mines within five miles of the village. The Slapewath Mine opened in 1864, and one of the shafts reached a depth of 286 feet (87m). However, all of the mines had closed by 1964.

From Slapewath the route crosses the summit of Airy Hill and descends gradually to Skelton Green before continuing through the fields to Skelton-in-Cleveland. Shortly after the Norman Conquest, Richard de Surdeval built a timber castle at Skelton c.1072-5, this fortified enclosure or 'burgus' had a church and a small feudal village. The 'burgus' occupied a peninsula surrounded by a dry defensive moat, 240 feet (73m) wide and 50 feet (15m) in depth, which took advantage of the natural ravines and slopes. Robert de Brus II rebuilt the castle in stone c.1140; it had two towers, dungeons and a moat with a drawbridge and portcullis. In 1788 John Wharton demolished the old castle, which had fallen into a state of disrepair, and also took down the man-made promontory on which it stood and had the moat filled in. The present Skelton Castle dates from 1794 and is a Gothic-style castellated mansion fronted by a lake.

The Cleveland Way weaves through the streets of Skelton and continues across the fields to reach Crow Wood. After passing beneath an impressive railway viaduct, we follow Skelton Beck to Saltburn. The Riftswood Viaduct built c.1872, stands 783 feet (238m) in height. The line maintained a passenger service until 1958.

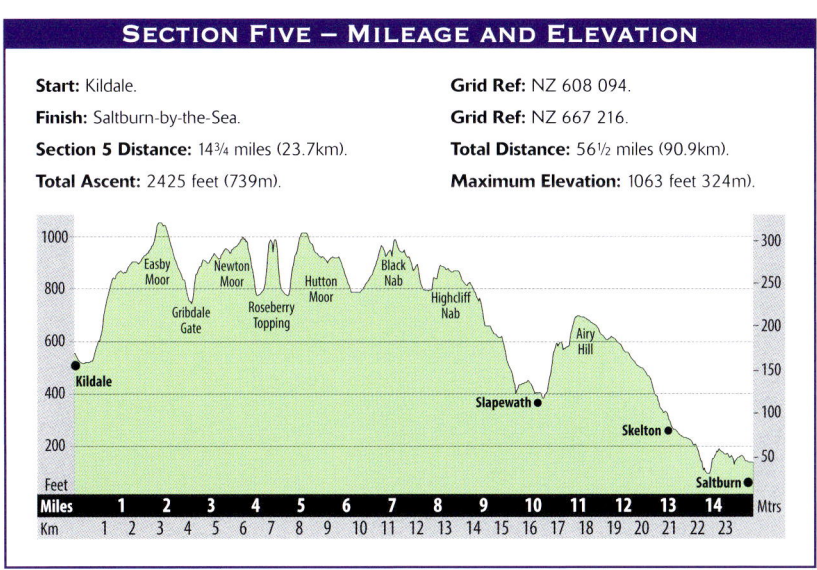

SECTION FIVE – MILEAGE AND ELEVATION

Start: Kildale.
Finish: Saltburn-by-the-Sea.
Section 5 Distance: 14¾ miles (23.7km).
Total Ascent: 2425 feet (739m).

Grid Ref: NZ 608 094.
Grid Ref: NZ 667 216.
Total Distance: 56½ miles (90.9km).
Maximum Elevation: 1063 feet 324m).

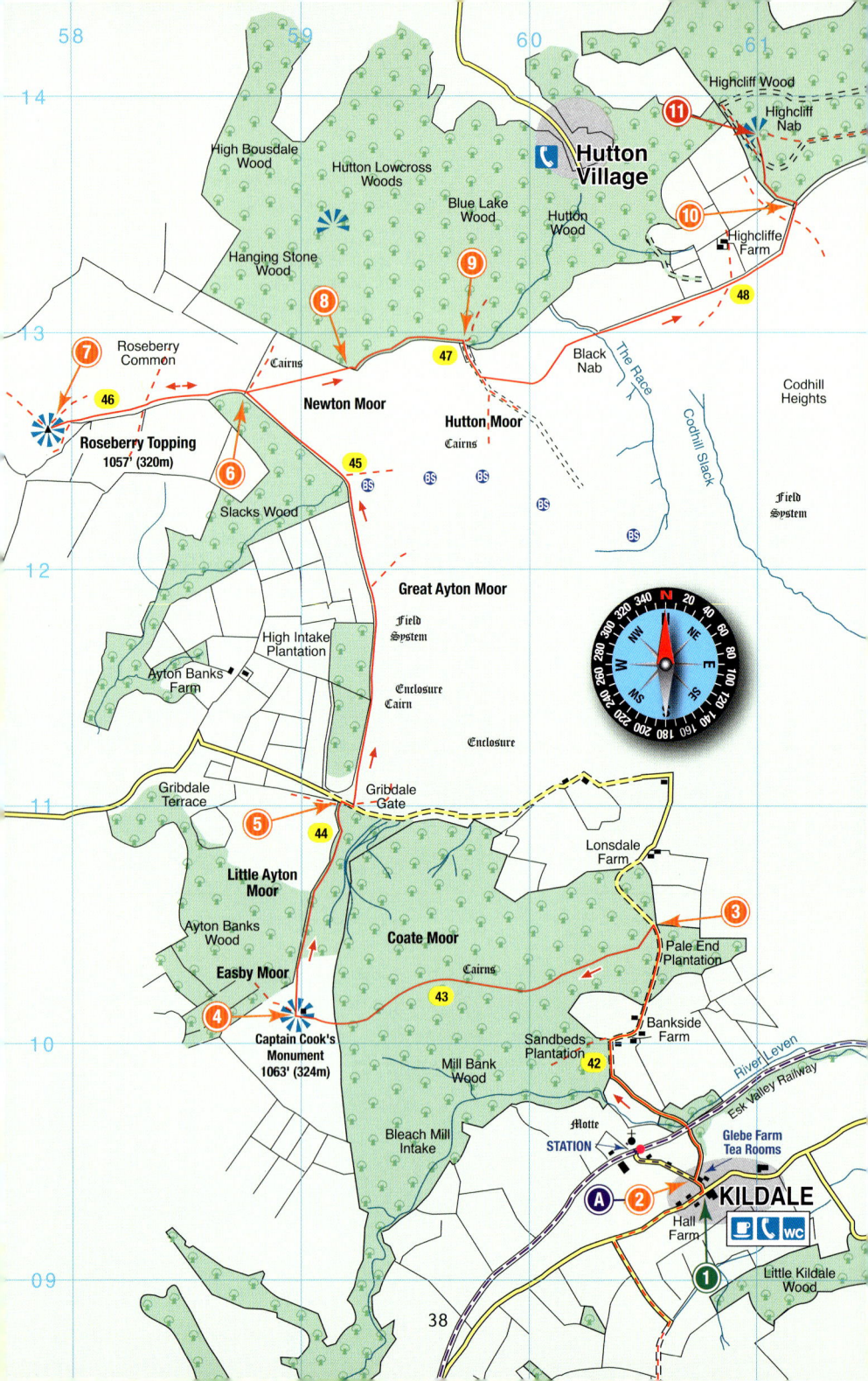

Map 14
Kildale to Highcliff Nab

① **608094** Turn left *(Station Road)* and follow the road into the village to the junction at the Glebe Farm Tea Rooms.

Ⓐ **607094** To visit St Cuthbert's Church, follow the road over the railway line. Afterwards, retrace steps to the Glebe Farm Tea Rooms and follow directions given in point 2.

② **607094** Turn right *(Waymark)* and follow the road, passing under the railway bridge. Continue along the road ascending to Bankside Farm and into the Pale End Plantation.

③ **605105** Turn Left *(SP Cleveland Way - Gribdale 2 miles)* and follow a clear track ascending through the wood. After leaving the wood continue through the heather to the Cook Monument.

④ **590101** After passing the monument turn right *(Waymark)*, begin descending on a paved path, and then a rough track leads through a gate to the road at Gribdale Gate. **CAUTION: busy road!**

⑤ **592110** Turn right and follow the road for about 30 yards (27m). Leave the road *(SP Cleveland Way)* and follow a track heading off to the left. Ascend a stepped path and then continue along the left boundary to point 6.

⑥ **588127** Go through the gate, turn left and continue alongside the boundary. Descend steeply via a paved path *(very slippery in wet conditions)*. Continue along the edge of Roseberry Common and join another stone path which leads uphill to the summit of Roseberry Topping.

⑦ **579126** Return via the outward route to point 6 and after passing through the gate head diagonally across Newton Moor *(Waymark)* and into Hanging Stone Wood.

⑧ **592128** Go through the gate, turn right *(Waymark)* and follow the right boundary to a gate.

⑨ **597130** Pass through the gate, turn right and continue through two more gates. Follow a broad track for about 200 yards (194m). Turn left and continue on a paved path beside the wall to Highcliff Wood.

⑩ **612135** Go through a gate *(SP Cleveland Way)* and follow a rough track through the wood. Cross a broad track *(Waymark)* and ascend along a narrow path to Highcliff Nab. Turn right *(Waymark)* and climb some steps leading to the summit.

⑪ **610138** Route directions continue from **MAP 15 – POINT 11.**

Roseberry Topping

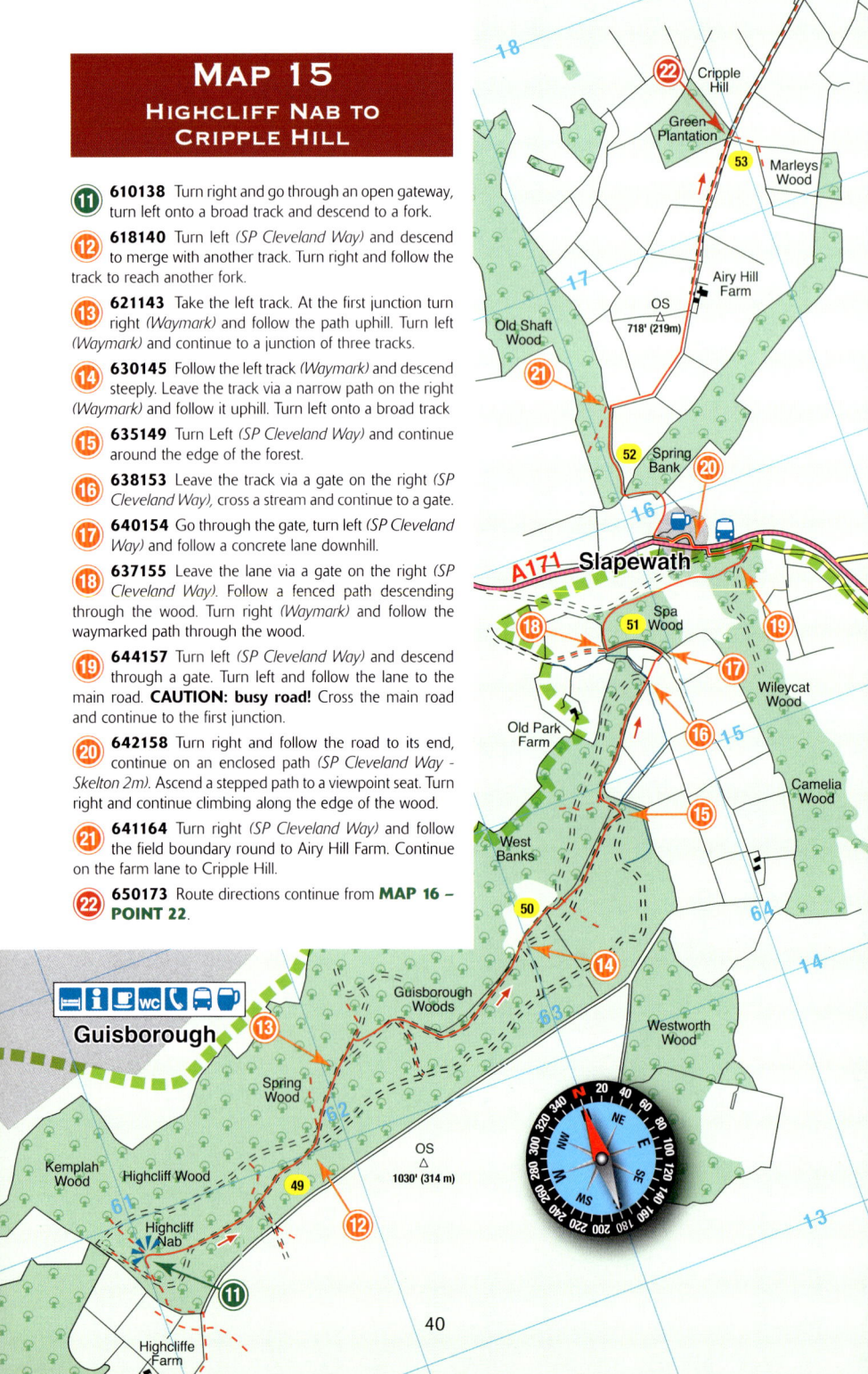

Map 16
Cripple Hill to Saltburn-by-the-Sea

(22) 650173 Follow the farm lane to Skelton Green *(near Manless Terrace)*.

(23) 657181 Continue straight ahead along Airy Hill Lane *(SP Cleveland Way - Skelton ½m)* and follow it to the main road. **CAUTION: busy road!** Cross the road and go through the gate opposite *(SP Cleveland Way)*. Now follow a fenced tarmac path through the fields.

(24) 657187 Turn right and follow the road to a bench seat. Leave the road via a path on the left *(SP Cleveland Way)* and descend into a car park. Continue across the High Street **CAUTION: busy road!** Descend into Coniston Road.

(25) 658189 Turn right into Derwent Road *(SP Cleveland Way)*, follow it around, and descend to the bottom. Continue into the cul-de-sac and go through an opening in the fence.

(26) 659193 Bear half left, heading diagonally across the field and pass through a gap in a large hedge. Continue across Bowland Road and follow a fenced path between the housing *(SP Cleveland Way - Saltburn 1m)*. Go through a gateway *(Waymark)* and pass underneath the A174 leading into Crow Wood.

(27) 659197 Follow a clear track leading into a large field. Keep to the right boundary around the field and re-enter Crow Wood. Continue on a good track and descend some steps to reach Skelton Beck, turn right and follow the beck downstream to a footbridge.

(28) 661201 Cross the footbridge and turn right. Pass beneath the Riftswood Viaduct. Continue downstream, turn left *(Waymark)* and follow a broad enclosed track uphill to a junction.

(29) 663203 Leave the track via a path on the right and enter the Saltburn Valley Gardens *(SP Cleveland Way)*. Follow the waymarked track through the wood to the bend of a tarmac lane.

(30) 665208 Bear left *(SP Cleveland Way - Saltburn Town Centre)* and after a few yards turn left *(SP Cleveland Way)*. Follow the path to some steps leading onto the main road.

(31) 665211 Turn right *(SP Cleveland Way)* and follow the road to the seafront. **CAUTION: busy road!**

(32) 667216 Route directions continue from **MAP 17 – POINT 1**.

Refreshments and accommodation are available at both Skelton and Saltburn.

The Heritage Coast

Yorkshire's Jurassic Park

Between Saltburn and Scalby Mills, the Cleveland Way follows the entire length of the North Yorkshire and Cleveland Heritage Coast. There are more than forty designated Heritage Coasts around the coastline of England and Wales; a designation which gives special protection to delicate areas of the coast, ensuring that they remain unexploited by industry and tourism.

Here the coastline embraces an area of beautiful and unspoilt countryside, comprising small fishing villages, towering cliffs with steep wooded valleys and sheltered bays with golden sandy beaches. Popularly known as the Dinosaur Coast, this dramatic coastline is internationally famous for its geological exposures and rich fossil resources. Due to the instability of the sea cliffs, the shoreline continually changes and just about everywhere along the coast from Saltburn to Scarborough, fossils are prolific in the exposed rocks. These rocks formed during the Jurassic period, between 200 and 145 million years ago and contain the fossilised remains of the plants and animals from that time, and dinosaur footprints!

The most common fossils found hereabouts are ammonites, sometimes called snakestones owing to their likeness to coiled serpents. According to a local legend, ammonites originated when the Abbess Hilda of Whitby, later St Hilda, drove a plague of snakes over the cliff at Whitby, and one species of ammonite, named Hildoceras, honours this mythical act. Furthermore, there are footprints of three-toed carnivorous theropods and plant-eating sauropods which once roamed the mudflats in search of food. In 2015 part of the vertebra belonging to a sauropod fell out of a cliff face near Whitby, which experts have since identified as being Britain's oldest sauropod dinosaur dating back about 176 million years. The sauropods had distinctive long necks and tails with small heads and a large body. Some species grew up to 115 feet (35m) long, possibly weighing up to 80 tonnes; the largest land animals that have ever lived on Earth.

Besides fossils, the Heritage Coast also has many sites of archaeological interest, testifying to man's impact on the landscape. Between the seventeenth and nineteenth centuries, mining and quarrying removed vast quantities of alum, ironstone and jet from the coastal cliffs. Consequently, the scars left behind by these enterprises are visible today on a number of the headlands, including Kettleness, Sandsend and Saltwick.

During the Roman occupation, watchtowers were built on the cliff tops to warn against the threat of Anglo-Saxon raids. The towers signalled to land-based patrols to prepare them for the attack. The cliff tops were once again pressed into service during World War II with the construction of reinforced concrete pillboxes and anti-tank cubes along the coastline. Some of the features from these periods remain on the shores and cliff tops.

Heritage Coast stone marker

Saltburn-by-the-Sea

A Victorian Bathing Resort

Frequently called Teesside's 'Jewel in the Crown', Saltburn-by-the-Sea provides visitors with an authentic seaside experience. The town evolved during the Victorian period, and their passion for seaside resorts created some of its most striking features.

The name derives from the Anglo-Saxon 'Sealt-Burna', meaning 'salty stream', their name for the stream now called Skelton Beck. Nevertheless, in medieval times 'salt panning' did take place near the beck's outlet. The process of salt panning uses shallow artificial basins to trap seawater, and after reducing it by evaporation to brine, it crystallises into salt for harvesting.

Much of Saltburn's charm as a Victorian seaside resort extends its appeal to the visitors of today, including the colourful Italian Gardens, a miniature railway and its beautiful golden sands. The town also boasts one of the world's oldest water balanced inclined tramways. Saltburn's tramway opened in 1884 to replace an earlier vertical cliff hoist. Its two cars, each fitted with a large water tank beneath, travel on parallel tracks. The weight of the top car is increased by adding water to its tank until it outweighs that of the lower car. At this point, gravity takes over allowing the top car to descend to the bottom, and the process begins all over again by recycling the water to the top. A brakeman controls the entire operation from his cabin at the top of the incline. The tramway links the town to its resplendent pleasure pier; the last surviving iron pier on England's north-east coastline.

When it opened in May 1869, Saltburn Pier was 1500 feet (457m) long and had a landing stage for paddle-steamers. During the first six months, more than fifty thousand people paid to stroll along it. Unfortunately, in October 1875 a storm destroyed the

Saltburn's Tramway and Pier

pier-head landing stage and a section of the deck, reducing its length to 1250 feet (381m). Throughout its long history, the pier has had to close several times for repairs due to storm damage. Moreover, in May 1924 the SS *Ovenbeg* crashed into the structure causing a 210-foot (64m) gap, subsequently repaired. But the most significant threat came in 1975 when the council applied for a demolition order. However, a 'Save the Pier' campaign led to a public inquiry which decided that only the last thirteen piles should be removed, reducing the pier's length to 681 feet (208m). The pier is still a major attraction for visitors, and in 2009 the National Piers Society voted it 'Pier of the Year'.

Saltburn-by-the-Sea to Runswick Bay
Section Six – 12 miles (19.3km)

The railway line along Hunt Cliff

This section provides an excellent introduction to the beautiful coastline of the nationally significant Heritage Coast. The route reveals sandy beaches and sheltered bays, rocky shorelines and towering cliffs, and visits the picturesque villages of Staithes and Runswick Bay.

Within a few minutes of leaving Saltburn, we are walking along the cliff-top to Hunt Cliff. The cliff face hereabouts supports colonies of kittiwake, and during the breeding season you will hear an unmistakable 'kitti-waak' call. Kittiwakes live out at sea feeding on small fish and squid, and they only come ashore to breed.

In summer, swathes of wildflowers bathe the cliff top with colour. The coastal grasslands sustain the scarce dyer's greenweed and three species of orchid, as well as other plants, including sea plantain, spiny restharrow and wild carrot.

Further along the cliff, an information point records that a Roman signal station existed near here. Excavations in 1911-12 unearthed coins dating from AD 362-392 as well as brooches, sandals, wooden bowls, pottery and a jet finger ring. Unfortunately, due to erosion, all traces of the site have since disappeared. The signal station at Hunt Cliff was one of several sited along the Yorkshire coast, which served as watchtowers to signal land-based patrols, warning them against the threat of Anglo-Saxon raids from Denmark and Germany. The turret was 50 feet (15.2m) long, and the walls were 7½ feet (2.3m) thick indicating that these defences also served as fortifications, in addition to signalling.

The railway line passing close to the edge of Hunt Cliff is the remains of the former Whitby, Redcar and Middlesbrough Union Railway, authorised by an Act of Parliament in 1866. Moreover, the line followed a very scenic coastal route and was open to passenger traffic between 1875 and 1958 linking communities along the east coast. However, these days the railway serves the sole purpose of transporting goods and materials to and from the Boulby Potash Mine near Staithes. The buildings beside the line are the remains of the Guibal Fanhouse, which provided vital ventilation to the Huntcliffe Ironstone Mine.

From Hunt Cliff, we return to sea level at Cattersty Sands, which has a long beach with clear water, beautiful sands and rocks at either end. The path leads to Skinningrove which was formerly a fishing community. However, in 1848 Cleveland's first ironstone mine opened at Skinningrove, being the first of eighty-three ironstone mines in the region. The mine workings now serve as the Cleveland Ironstone Mining Museum, which celebrates the legacy of ironstone mining and the broader industrial heritage of Cleveland. In 1874 a forge opened nearby, and the village expanded rapidly to accommodate the demand for iron. The ironworks supplied steel for building bridges and railways across Europe, America, Africa, India and Australia. More recently, Skinningrove provided 3500 tonnes of special steel profiles for the aircraft carrier, HMS *Queen Elizabeth* the largest warship ever built for the Royal Navy.

Leaving Skinningrove, the path climbs steadily to Boulby Cliffs, which are the highest cliffs on the east coast of England standing 666 feet (203m) at Rock Cliff. The views along the coastline are exhilarating, although the landscape below is more austere, and bears the marks of the many quarries left behind by the alum and ironstone industries.

After descending from Boulby, we continue beside Cowbar Lane, which drops steeply downhill to the picturesque fishing village of Staithes, which merits further exploration *(see page 49)*. At Staithes the Cleveland Way formerly climbed away from the cliff edge before rising steeply through the fields to cross the slopes of Beacon Hill. However, the route now utilises a stretch of the England Coast Path, which takes walkers closer to the cliff edge and allows superb views of Staithes, the harbour and Cowbar Nab. The England Coast Path will eventually follow the entire coast of England, and when completed, will be the world's longest coastal path, covering a total distance of around 2795 miles (4498km).

Shortly after passing some former coastguard cottages the forlorn old jetty at Port Mulgrave appears below. The harbour at Port Mulgrave opened in 1857, and it enabled cheap transportation of iron ore from the local mines to the Jarrow blast furnaces on Tyneside, which produced steel for the shipbuilding industry. Much of the ore came from the Grinkle ironstone mine 3 miles (5km) inland, and it travelled on a narrow-gauge railway which crossed three wooden viaducts and passed through two tunnels to reach the harbour. During World War I, ships leaving the port were in danger of attack as iron was a vital resource. Therefore in 1916, an incline was constructed to connect the Grinkle mine to the Whitby, Redcar and Middlesbrough Union Railway and Port Mulgrave became redundant.

Just a few more miles along the cliff tops leads to beautiful Runswick Bay. Although this stage ends at the bay, if you're staying elsewhere, you could finish at Runswick Bank Top, delaying the steep climb (both ways) to the start of section seven.

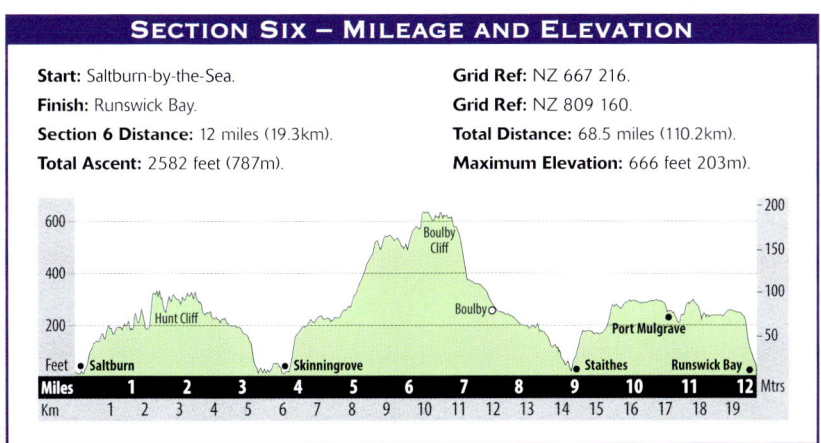

SECTION SIX – MILEAGE AND ELEVATION

Start: Saltburn-by-the-Sea.
Finish: Runswick Bay.
Section 6 Distance: 12 miles (19.3km).
Total Ascent: 2582 feet (787m).

Grid Ref: NZ 667 216.
Grid Ref: NZ 809 160.
Total Distance: 68.5 miles (110.2km).
Maximum Elevation: 666 feet 203m).

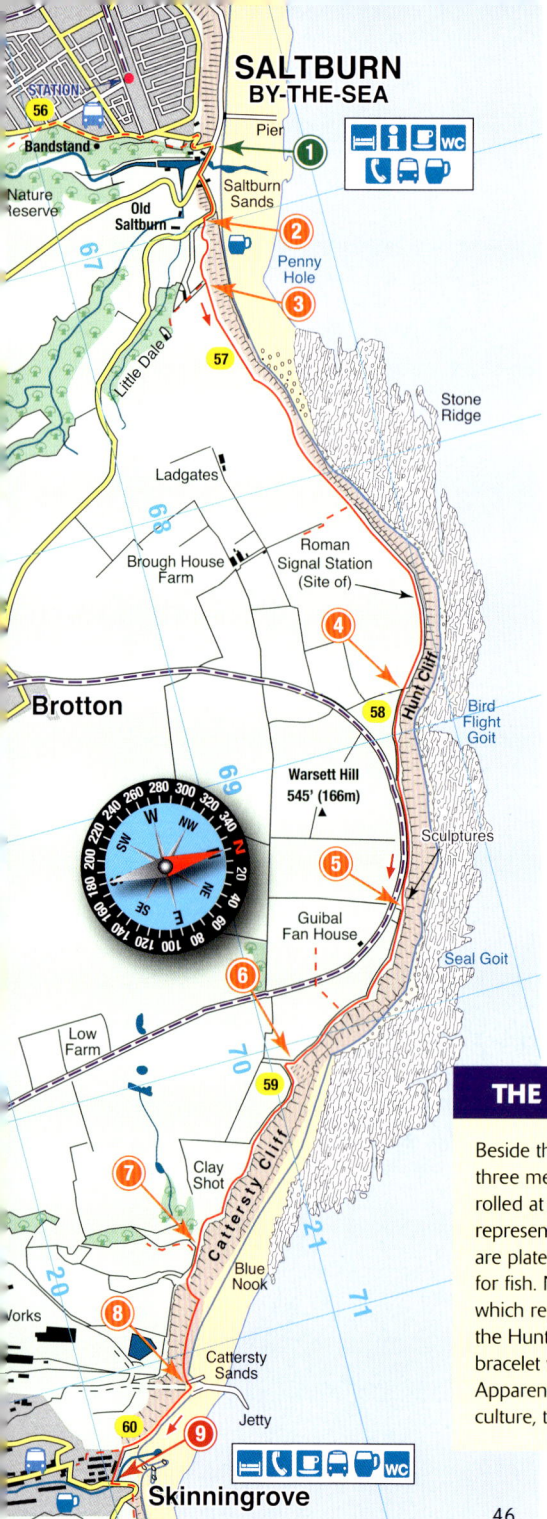

MAP 17
SALTBURN-BY-THE-SEA TO SKINNINGROVE

① **667216** Turn right and follow the road along the seafront, passing to the right of the Ship Inn.

② **670215** After passing the inn, leave the road via a track on the left *(SP Cleveland Way - Skinningrove 3.5m)*. Ascend a stepped path to the cliff top.

③ **672215** Continue along the edge of Hunt Cliff, passing the site of a Roman signal station.

④ **688218** Go through the gate and head towards the railway line. Follow a clear path beside the line, passing some steel sculptures.

⑤ **696216** Bear left and descend to the left of an enclosure *(NT Warsett Hill)*. Continue along the cliff top.

⑥ **701211** Turn right and follow an enclosed path for a short distance. Turn left through a gap in the hedge and return to the cliff top. Begin a gradual descent along Cattersty Cliff.

⑦ **706205** Descend a steep path to a signpost. Turn left *(SP Cleveland Way)* and descend a stepped path towards the beach, and then follow a sandy path to the old jetty.

⑧ **711204** Go through a gap in the jetty, bear right and follow a broad track to Skinningrove. Turn left *(SP Cleveland Way)* and follow the road to a bridge.

⑨ **714200** Route directions now continue from **MAP 18 – POINT 9**.

Refreshments, accommodation and toilets are available at Skinningrove.

THE HUNT CLIFF SCULPTURES

Beside the railway line on Hunt Cliff, there are three metal sculptures, produced from steel rolled at Skinningrove. First, the Trawl Door which represents the local fishing industry – trawl doors are plates used to keep nets open while trawling for fish. Next, the Pillar with four shapes attached, which represent earth, air, sky and water. Finally, the Huntcliff Circle, which resembles a charm bracelet with ten charms suspended from the top. Apparently, each charm represents a story of local culture, tradition or folklore.

MAP 18
SKINNINGROVE TO BOULBY

9 **714200** Turn left *(SP Cleveland Way)* and follow the road around the right bend. Leave the road *(SP Cleveland Way - Boulby 3.5m)* and climb a steep stone path to the hilltop. Continue to Hummersea Bank.

10 **725198** At a junction of paths go straight across *(SP Cleveland Way - Staithes 4m)* and continue along the cliff, climbing gradually.

11 **729198** Turn right *(SP Cleveland Way)* and climb up to a farm track. Turn left *(SP Cleveland Way)* and follow the track to Warren Farm.

12 **731197** Head to the right of the garage and cross the farmyard. Go through a gate *(SP Cleveland Way)*. Continue uphill, go through another gate *(NT Loftus Alum Quarries)*. Cross two small footbridges.

13 **735198** At a waymark, follow the right track *(Acorn symbol)*. Continue uphill and follow the waymarks, passing above the old alum quarries. Continue above the workings along the cliff top.

14 **743199** Descend to the right and follow the wall round *(re-entering the National Park)*. Climb back up and follow the path through a kissing gate to Rock Cliff *(Information Point)*. Continue along the cliff top.

15 **754193** Bear left slightly and begin a steep descent. Go through a gate and continue descending into Boulby. Follow the road to a right hand bend.

16 **763189** Route directions now continue from **MAP 19 – POINT 16**.

BOULBY POTASH MINE

At 4600 feet (1400m) deep, the Boulby Potash Mine is the second deepest mine in Europe. It has a network of underground roads which extend 3.1 miles (5km) under the North Sea, and cover a total distance of 620 miles (1000km). Because of its depth Boulby is a special place for science – 'a quiet place in the Universe' – where studies can be carried out almost entirely free of interference from natural background radiation.

MAP 19
BOULBY TO RUNSWICK BAY

16 **763189** Leave the road and follow an enclosed track *(SP Cleveland Way)*. Cross a large field and return to the cliff top.

17 **770187** Turn right and after a few yards turn left onto a tarmac lane *(SP Cleveland Way)*. Follow the lane, and a diverted section of the trail to Cowbar, *(permanent diversion due to a landslip)*. Turn left and descend along the road to a footbridge.

18 **782189** Cross the footbridge which leads into Staithes. Turn left and continue to the harbour.

19 **783188** Turn right into Church Street, continue uphill onto an enclosed track *(SP Port Mulgrave 1m)*. Keep left at a fork and ascend to Fulwood Farm.

20 **785186** Turn left and go through a gate *(SP Cleveland Way)*. Follow a fenced path to the cliff edge. Turn right and continue around the cliff top to a gate.

21 **792184** Go through the gate, turn left and follow the fence uphill. Pass through another gate *(SP Cleveland Way)* and continue to the road near the former coastguard station at Port Mulgrave.

22 **796175** Leave the road and follow a clear path along the cliff top *(SP Cleveland Way Runswick Bay 2m)*.

23 **810165** Turn right and follow a clear track to Runswick Bank Top. Turn left *(SP Cleveland Way)* and follow the road to the Cliffmount Hotel.

24 **808161** Continue between some concrete posts *(SP Cleveland Way)* and descend a steep path leading to Runswick Bay. Turn left *(SP Cleveland Way)* and descend to a mini roundabout.

25 **809160** Route directions now continue from **MAP 20 – POINT 1.**

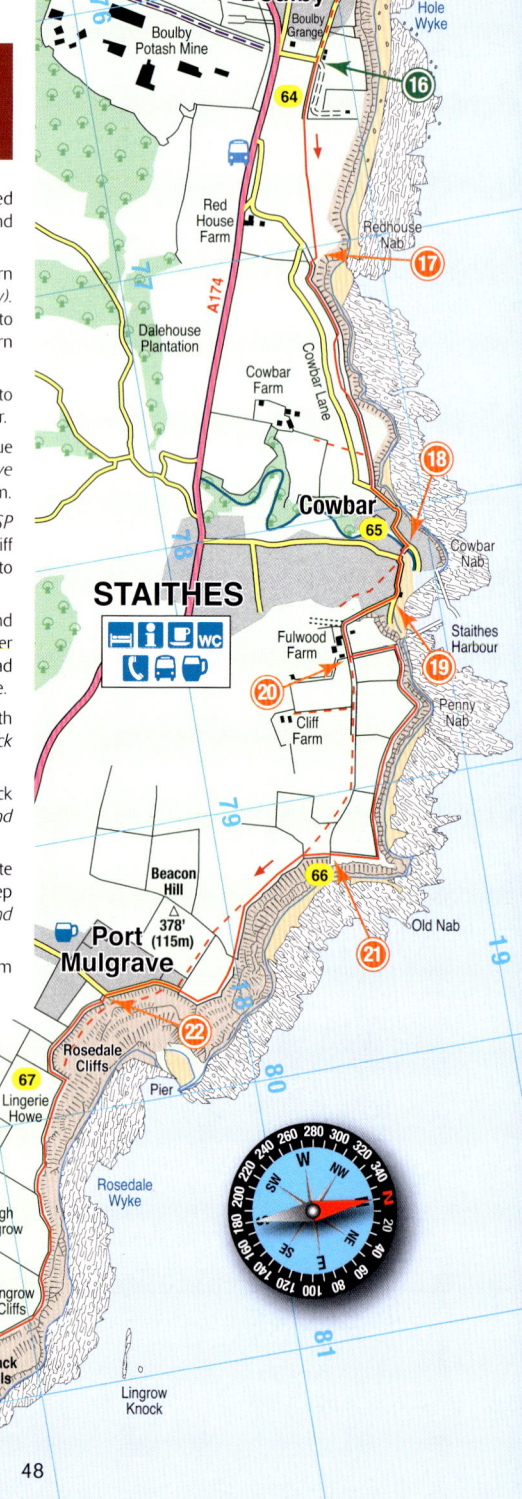

48

Staithes

A PROSPEROUS FISHING PORT

Staithes and Cowbar Nab

Staithes, pronounced as 'steers' by the locals, derives its name from 'staithe' which means 'a landing place'. The village was formerly one of the largest fishing ports on the north-east coast of the UK.

At the beginning of the twentieth century, eighty full-time fishing boats were putting out from Staithes. More than a century later the port still has a few part-time fishermen and it maintains a small fleet of traditional cobles. The distinctive shape of a coble is flat-bottomed with a high bow, and it possibly originates from a Viking design. The flat bottoms enabled boats to launch from and land onto shallow, sandy beaches. Moreover, fishing vessels required high bows to sail on the hazardous North Sea, especially when they were launching into the surf.

The harbour nestles between the bulky headlands of Cowbar Nab and Penny Nab with two long breakwaters to reduce the force of the waves and provide much-needed protection to the village. Despite being destroyed by fierce storms and rebuilt on at least three occasions, the Cod and Lobster Inn on the quayside continues to resist the wrath of the North Sea. The great storm of January 1953 washed away the front of the pub. Hopefully, improved sea defences will help to prevent that from happening again.

In 1744 James Cook arrived in Staithes to begin his haberdashery apprenticeship in the shop of William Sanderson. But It was not long before 16-year-old James became fascinated by seafaring tales and of becoming a seaman, and Sanderson realised that the youngster's heart was not in shopkeeping. Furthermore, in July 1746 he found Cook an apprenticeship in the Merchant Navy with Whitby shipowner Captain John Walker, thus starting his incredible maritime career.

Additional information about Cook's time in Staithes is available at the Captain Cook and Staithes Heritage Centre, housed in the old Methodist chapel. The museum has a complete re-creation of Sanderson's shop and is overflowing with exhibits from the life and voyages of the great seafarer.

Further exploration of the village reveals an intriguing network of alleys and ginnels, which bear curious names such as Gun Gutter, Slip Top and Dog Loup. The latter is the narrowest street in the UK, and at a mere 18 inches (457mm) in width, stouter walkers may have to shed a few pounds if they wish to pass through it!

Runswick Bay to Robin Hood's Bay
SECTION SEVEN – 15¼ MILES (24.5KM)

From Runswick Bay, the trail returns to the cliff tops, and the coastal scenery is outstanding. At Sandsend, why not take a paddle in the sea to refresh those tired feet? The halfway point is Whitby, which makes the ideal place for lunch with its many cafés and pubs. After ascending the 199 steps to Whitby Abbey, the trail undulates along the cliff top to Robin Hood's Bay.

Old anchor, Runswick Bay

The idyllic village of Runswick Bay nestles at the northern end of a beautiful sandy beach, protected by the towering cliff of Lingrow Knowle and some grey stone sea walls. Its narrow pedestrian lanes weave their way between the cottages and houses, and on the seafront, the former coastguard's cottage is the only remaining thatched house on the Yorkshire coast. In 1682 a landslide swept away the entire village except for one cottage. Nevertheless, there were no casualties because most of the community were attending a funeral wake. One of the mourners realised what was happening and raised the alarm to evacuate the village. Allegedly, the house that survived belonged to the dead man!

Unless the tides are very high, the beach path should be passable. However, beware the caves at Hob Holes, one of which, according to local legend is the home of the 'Hob of Hob Hole'. In Yorkshire folklore, hobs, goblins, boggles and boggarts are unfriendly sprites with a mischievous nature. But the occupant of the Hob Hole cave had healing powers and could cure a whooping cough. Apparently, villagers carried their sick children into the cave and asked for help by the uttering of a rhyme. No one knows what became of the 'Hob of Hob Hole', although some locals still claim that they've seen him lurking around Runswick Bay.

After ascending to High Cliff, we continue along the cliff top to Kettleness. The path passes around the headland and follows a short section of the old Lofthouse to Whitby railway line which opened in 1883 and closed in 1958. The designated course of the line was along the cliff top. Unfortunately, part of the cliff collapsed into the sea during construction, and the only alternative was to tunnel through the headlands. The Kettleness tunnel is 308 yards (282m) in length, and after emerging from the cliff, an open section of the track once linked it to the Sandsend tunnel which is 1652 yards (1.51km) long. Please do not attempt to enter either of the tunnels – they are unsafe and have not received any maintenance since the line closed in 1958.

The Cleveland Way continues along the cliff top to Telgreen Hill, where we drop down into Overdale Wood, and after a much steeper descent through the wood, we rejoin the railway trackbed near the entrance to the Sandsend Tunnel. The level trackbed winds its way passed the former Deepgrove and Sandsend Alum Quarries. Evidently this bleak wasteland, after being appropriately whitened by computer graphics, appeared as the Antarctic landscape in the 2012 film *Shackleton* which starred Sir Kenneth Branagh.

At Sandsend, unless the tide is receding, it's safer to follow the promoted route along the road to the Captain Cook statue on Whitby's West Cliff. Whether your interests lie in history and culture, vampires and Goths, or just fish and chips – Whitby ticks all the boxes. Finding sufficient time to savour its many delights is the only problem! The town is probably most famous for its fishing and whaling fleets, and the celebrated explorer Captain James Cook, who began his legendary naval career in Whitby *(see page 58)*. Furthermore, the Irish author Bram Stoker conceived the idea for his classic novel *Dracula* in Whitby.

In 1890 while staying at a guesthouse in Whitby, Bram Stoker read about the shipwreck of a Russian vessel named the *Dmitry*, from Narva. The ship ran aground in 1885 on Tate Hill Sands carrying a cargo of silvery sand. After a slight modification of the name, this became the *Demeter* from Varna which brings Dracula to Whitby with a shipment of silver sand and boxes of earth from Transylvania. Immediately after the *Demeter* ran aground, an enormous black dog leapt ashore and bounded up the 199 steps towards Whitby Abbey – Dracula had arrived! However, Stoker spent six more years researching the scenery and traditions of Transylvania, and the name of his villain, before publishing his novel. Nevertheless, his holiday in Whitby inspired some of the novel's most dramatic scenes.

From the West Cliff, we pass through a whalebone arch and descend to the harbourside, and after crossing the swing bridge into the old town, we have to contend with the 199 steps, known locally as the Church Stairs. Every tenth step and the last

Cædmon Cross

one has a small brass plate denoting the step number – so there's no need to count them! At the top of the steps, in the graveyard of St Mary's Church, stands the Cædmon Cross, erected in 1898 to commemorate the talented seventh-century poet. According to Bede, Cædmon was a lay brother at Whitby Abbey, where he cared for the animals. One evening, while the monks were feasting and singing, Cædmon left early to sleep because he knew nothing about the art of song. But, while asleep, he had a vision, and after he awoke, composed a short poem praising God and the creation, which he sang to the Abbess Hilda. Subsequently, the abbess took Cædmon into the monastic community where he became an enthusiastic monk and a skilful and inspirational Christian poet.

The Abbess Hilda, also known as Hild and later St Hilda, was a Northumbrian princess; she founded the first monastery here in AD 657. The abbey soon became one of the most revered religious centres in the Anglo-Saxon world. In AD 664 it was the setting for the Synod of Whitby, to decide whether the Church should adopt the Celtic or Roman method for calculating the date of the movable Easter feast. The synod voted in favour of the Roman system which contributed to a decline in Celtic Christianity – a landmark in the history of the Church in England.

Whitby Abbey

During the late ninth century, the monastery and the surrounding area became abandoned, possibly as a result of Viking raids. In c.1078 after a lapse of two centuries Reinfrid, a Benedictine monk who had been a valiant soldier in the army of William the Conqueror, founded a new monastic community. However, in 1539 the crown confiscated Whitby Abbey and all its possessions during the Dissolution of the Monasteries under Henry VIII. Further, in December 1914 German battleships shelled Whitby and the abbey sustained considerable damage to the west front.

From the abbey, we continue along the cliff top to Saltwick Bay. In October 1914, the hospital ship SS *Rohilla* sank in the bay near Saltwick Nab. The weather conditions made rescue extremely difficult, but 146 of the 229 on board survived, including the captain and all the nurses. Moreover, one of the survivors was Mary Kezia Roberts; she had survived the sinking of RMS *Titanic* just two years earlier in 1912.

Apart from a couple of small valleys, the rest of today's route is relatively undemanding and clings to the cliff top all the way to Robin Hood's Bay.

SECTION SEVEN – MILEAGE AND ELEVATION

Start: Runswick Bay.
Finish: Robin Hood's Bay.
Section 7 Distance: 15¼ miles (24.5km).
Total Ascent: 2704 feet (824m).

Grid Ref: NZ 809 160.
Grid Ref: NZ 953 049.
Total Distance: 83¾ miles (134.8km).
Maximum Elevation: 369 feet (113m).

MAP 20
RUNSWICK BAY TO DEEPGROVE WYKE

① **809160** Bear right down the boat slipway leading to the beach and walk along the sands for about ½ mile (800m). **SEE PANEL →**

② **815154** After passing the buildings of the Runswick Bay Sailing Club turn right and follow Claymoor Beck into a break in the cliffs. Ascend on a stepped path and cross a wooden footbridge. Continue ascending to a welcoming viewpoint seat at High Cliff.

③ **817153** Continue uphill and follow the fence over the summit. Drop down slightly and then ascend to a gate.

④ **823154** Go through the gate and follow the left fence through two more gates. Cross a small dip and ascend some steps. Now continue along the fence to a gate.

⑤ **829155** Pass through the gate *(SP Cleveland Way)* and follow a farm track to the left. Keep to the left of the farm and head back to the cliff top. Bear right and follow the fence around the farm and onto the main road.

⑥ **831156** Turn left and follow the road for about 50 yards (45m). Leave the road via a track on the left *(SP Cleveland Way - Sandsend 3mls)*. Bear right and follow the right fence along the cliff top. Go through a gate and continue along the cliff top to the dismantled railway.

⑦ **838155** Cross a step stile and climb a few steps. Turn left *(SP Cleveland Way)* and follow the track over another step stile, *(passing above the Kettleness Tunnel entrance)*. The path now follows the cliff top to Telgreen Hill.

⑧ **851146** Leave the cliff top and follow the right wall downhill to the entrance of a wood.

⑨ **854142** Route directions continue from **MAP 21 – POINT 9.**

THE KETTLENESS DISASTER

The history of Kettleness further emphasises the instability of the coastal cliffs around here. On the night of 17th December 1829 torrential rain caused part of the cliff to slide gradually into the sea carrying the entire village with it. Fortunately, the villagers were able to take refuge on an alum ship anchored offshore, and there was no loss of life.

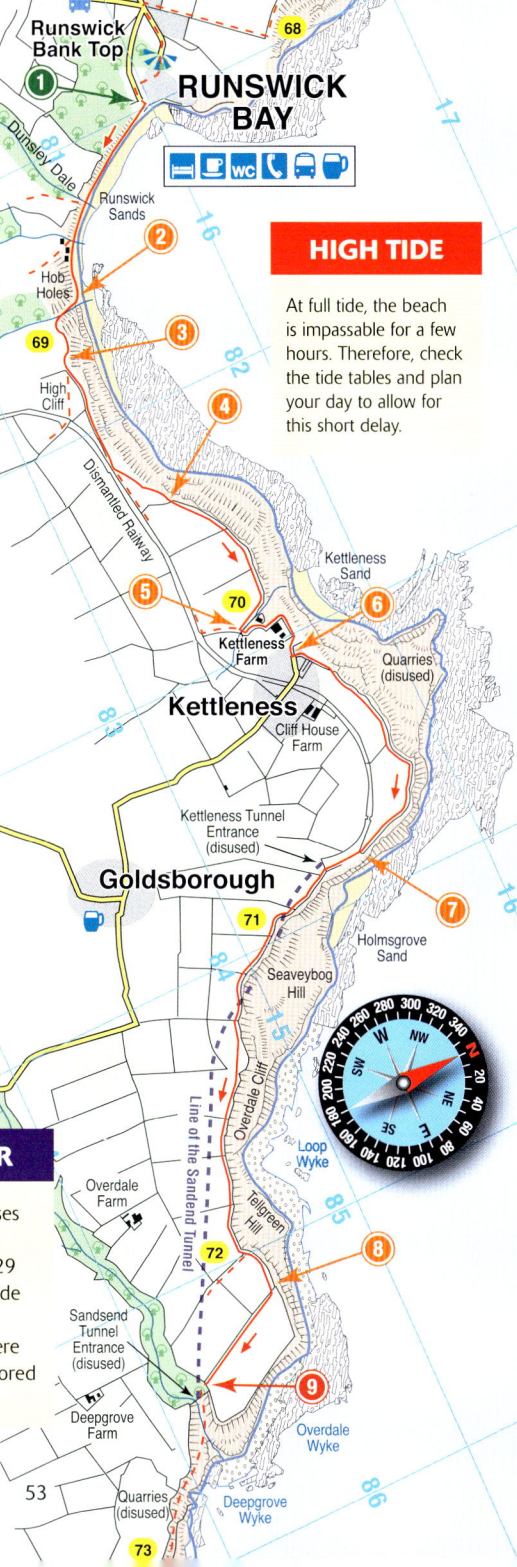

HIGH TIDE

At full tide, the beach is impassable for a few hours. Therefore, check the tide tables and plan your day to allow for this short delay.

Map 21
Deepgrove Wyke to Whitby West Cliff

9 **854142** Enter the wood via a gate and descend some steep wooden and stone steps. **CAUTION: the steps are very steep and often slippery!** Rejoin the dismantled railway track near the entrance to the Sandsend Tunnel. Follow the trackbed for about 1 mile (1.6km). *(Leaving the National Park).*

10 **859130** Leave the trackbed via a narrow path on the left and descend some steps into the car park at Sandsend. Turn right and continue to the car park entrance.

11 **860129** Turn left onto the A174 main road and follow it for about 1¼ miles (2km). **CAUTION: busy road!**

12 **879116** After passing the Whitby Golf Club leave the main road via a narrow lane on the left *(SP Cleveland Way).*

13 **881119** Bear right and ascend a narrower path leading to the cliff top. Continue on a good path along the cliff top and return to the road near West Cliff.

14 **893114** Follow the road to the Captain Cook statue overlooking the harbour.

15 **897114** Route directions continue from **MAP 22 – POINT 15**.

Refreshments, accommodation and toilets are available at Sandsend and Whitby.

THE BEACH ROUTE

The promoted route of the Cleveland Way follows the road, but if the tide is receding it's possible to walk along the beach most of the way to Whitby.

A **863215** Descend steps onto the sands, turn right and follow the beach to point **B**.

B **881119** Option to leave the beach here. Bear right and then left onto the concrete seawall. Follow the seawall (or the sands) to point **C**.

C **890116** Continue along the seawall passing some beach huts and ascend via the Spa Centre to the West Cliff near the Captain Cook memorial statue.

DOG RESTRICTIONS – from 1st May to 30th September, dogs are **NOT** permitted beyond point **C**. Therefore leave the seawall (or the sands) via the steps on the right and follow a zig-zag path to the cliff top. Turn left and continue to **POINT 14**.

54

MAP 22
WHITBY WEST CLIFF TO WIDDY HEAD

(15) 897114 Go through the Whalebone Arch and descend the path into the Khyber Pass. Turn left, follow the road downhill around a double bend and turn right onto Pier Road. Continue along the road beside the pier to the swing bridge at Bridge Street

(16) 899110 Cross the bridge and head along Bridge Street into the old town.

(17) 900111 Turn left into Church Street and follow the cobbled road. Turn right and ascend the 199 steps to St Mary's Church. Continue through the churchyard to the road near Whitby Abbey.

(18) 903113 Turn left *(SP Cleveland Way - Robin Hood's Bay 6½m)* and head towards the cliff top. Turn right and follow a fenced path along the cliff top.

(19) 912111 Descend a few steps *(re-entering the National Park)*, bear right and follow a rough track into the caravan park. Turn left and follow the road through the caravan park.

(20) 915107 Leave the road via a gate on the left *(SP Cleveland Way - Robin Hood's Bay 5m)*. Follow a good path along the cliff top to Whitestone Point.

(21) 926103 Continue along the cliff top passing the Whitby Fog Signal Station. **CAUTION: The cliff side of the path is unfenced from this point!**

(22) 928101 Turn right and climb up through a gate *(SP Cleveland Way)*. Cross the service road and climb up some steps. Go through a gate *(SP Cleveland Way)* and pass above the lighthouse. Continue along the cliff top to Widdy Head.

(23) 932095 Route directions continue from **MAP 23 – POINT 23**.

LIGHTHOUSE and FOGHORN

The lighthouse at Ling Hill, erected in 1858, was originally one of a pair of lights aligned north-south to show fixed lights over Whitby Rock. In 1902 Trinity House replaced one of the lighthouses with a foghorn, its nicknames include the 'Whitby Bull' and the 'Mad Bull'. The foghorn station is now a private home and, fortunately for the owners, non-operational!

MAP 23
WIDDY HEAD TO ROBIN HOOD'S BAY

(23) 932095 Continue along the cliff edge to a memorial seat for Colin Thompson.

(24) 934091 Descend some steps into a small wooded valley, cross a stream and ascend some more steps, returning to the cliff top. Continue across two similar valleys to reach Maw Wyke Hole. **CAUTION: The steps leading through these three small valleys are steep and often slippery!**

(25) 941082 (*The Coast to Coast footpath joins the Cleveland Way at this point*). Return to the cliff top and continue to NT Bay Ness.

(26) 952071 Bear right and descend steeply into the gulley. Cross a couple of footbridges, climb back up and follow the cliff top to a gate below the coastguard station.

(27) 959064 Pass through the gate, turn left and follow the fence. Go through another gate, turn right, ascend some steps and continue to a gate.

(28) 957059 Go through the gate and follow the left fence. Leave the field via a gate, turn right and continue through two more gates leading to the road at Robin Hood's Bay.

(29) 952055 Follow the road (*Mount Pleasant North*) to the B1447. Turn left and follow the road downhill, keep left at the roundabout and descend to the seafront near the Bay Hotel.

(30) 953049 Route directions continue from **MAP 24 – POINT 1**.

Refreshments, accommodation and toilets are available at Robin Hood's Bay.

COAST TO COAST

The 192 mile (309km) journey from the Irish Sea at St Bees ends at Robin Hood's Bay. Walkers head down the narrow streets to the slipway, pass the Bay Hotel and stride out across the sandy beach until the North Sea laps their boots.

It is a custom for Coast to Coast walkers to take a pebble from one coastline and throw it into the sea when they arrive at the other one.

Whitby

SHIPBUILDING AND WHALING

The harbour and the sea have been the focus of life in Whitby for many centuries; fishing, shipbuilding and whaling have all played a significant role in the town's prosperity.

Although Whitby still maintains a small fishing fleet, the strength of its economy now relies more on tourism rather than industry. However, during the latter part of the eighteenth century, Whitby was England's third largest shipbuilding centre after London and Newcastle, with eleven shipyards along the river Esk. Whitby's shipbuilding industry is especially famous for its collier-barks, known as Whitby Cats; three-masted sailing ships designed for carrying coal. These sturdy boats had flat-bottomed keels, enabling them to land on beaches to load and unload their cargoes, and also made repairs and maintenance simple. Furthermore, these features made them popular with the explorers of the day, including Captain Cook; all four of his vessels were Whitby built collier ships.

The whalebone arch on Whitby's West Cliff is a memorial to the whaling industry. The 15-foot jaw bones came from a bowhead whale, legally killed by Alaskan Inuits in 1996, and unveiled by Miss Alaska in 2003. Two other arches have stood on the same spot; in 1963 Norway presented Whitby with some 20-foot jawbones from a fin whale to replace the original arch, erected c.1853, which was in terrible condition.

In 1753 the first two ships of the newly formed Whitby Whaling Company set sail for Greenland. By 1795 Whitby had become a significant whaling port, with fifty-five vessels operating from the harbour. Large boiler houses along the quayside rendered the whale blubber into oil used for street lighting; or utilised in the production of candles, soap, margarine and paint.

Whalebone Arch, West Cliff

However, the introduction of gas lighting reduced the former demand for whale products, and by 1831 only one whaling ship remained. The end of Whitby's whaling trade came in 1837 and the last whaling ship to return to the harbour was empty.

In addition to its maritime history Whitby is also well-known for its high-quality jet; a hard, black variety of lignite, derived from fossilised wood, which has endured tremendous pressure over millions of years. Although the history of jet dates back to at least the Bronze Age, it was during the Victorian period that Whitby Jet achieved popularity. After the death of her consort, Prince Albert in 1861, Queen Victoria began an extended period of mourning. The Queen decreed that only jewellery fashioned from jet was acceptable to wear at Court, thus confirming jet's status as the material of choice for jewellery during times of mourning.

Captain James Cook

EXPLORER, CIRCUMNAVIGATOR AND CARTOGRAPHER

James Cook, the British navigator and explorer, rose from humble beginnings to become the most legendary seaman of his time. Moreover, he discovered and accurately charted the entire coastline of New Zealand and the Great Barrier Reef of Australia, and he was also the first person to explore the Antarctic region.

Born on 27th October 1728, at Marton-in-Cleveland, Yorkshire, James Cook was the son of a Scottish farm worker and grew up on a farm near Great Ayton, where he attended the village school. In 1744 James moved to Staithes as an apprentice in the shop of William Sanderson. However, it was not long before 16-year-old James became fascinated by seafaring tales and of becoming a seaman, and Sanderson realised that the youngster's heart was not in shopkeeping. Furthermore, in July 1746 he found Cook an apprenticeship in the Merchant Navy with Captain John Walker, a Quaker coal-shipper from Whitby.

During his three year apprenticeship, transporting coal to and from Whitby, James Cook became proficient in mathematics and navigation. In 1755 Captain Walker offered him a command, but Cook decided to join the Royal Navy instead, and within a month he was master's mate aboard HMS *Eagle*. Two years later, he became the master of HMS *Pembroke*, which played a significant role in charting the approaches to Quebec up the St. Lawrence River in Canada and led to the capture of Louisburg and Quebec.

James Cook's first voyage as an explorer began in 1768 when he left England in command of HM *Bark Endeavour*. Although his mission was to observe the transit of Venus across the face of the sun from Tahiti, he also had sealed orders instructing him to find the 'Great Southern Continent' for which

Captain Cook

he found no evidence. Nevertheless, his search led to the discovery of New Zealand and Australia. During his second voyage in 1772-75 Cook's ships crossed the Antarctic circle numerous times, but the intense cold forced them to turn back. However, he dispelled the myth of an undiscovered southern continent, and on his return to England, he became the first person to circumnavigate the world in both directions.

On his third and final voyage in 1776-79 Cook's primary objective was to search for the existence of an entrance to the North West Passage which linked the Atlantic and Pacific oceans. In January 1778 he discovered the Hawaiian Islands, naming them the Sandwich Islands after his patron the Earl of Sandwich. During his first visit to Hawaii, Cook received a warm welcome; the natives treated him and his crew with great respect, providing them with gifts and food. The Hawaiians would not trade for beads or mirrors, although metal fascinated them. Therefore, Cook purchased provisions for his ships with iron and nails. In February

1778 Cook sailed from Hawaii to the North American coast heading to Alaska in search of the North West Passage. Evidently Cook came to within 50 miles (80km) of the entrance, but thick ice floes and violent currents in the Bering Sea prevented him from locating it. The expedition sailed back to the warmer waters of the Hawaiian Islands, arriving there in December 1778 to prepare for another attempt the following season.

After making a circumnavigation of Hawaii, which took over a month, the ships dropped anchor in Kealakekua Bay on 16th January 1779. Over 1000 canoes came out to greet them; apparently, Cook's arrival had coincided with celebrations marking the Hawaiian religious festival of Makahiki to their fertility god – Lono. The Hawaiians seemingly treated Cook and his crew as gods during this second visit, until one of the crewmen died, revealing that they were just mere mortals and relationships became agitated. The expedition left the islands on 4th February 1779. However, high gales broke the foremast of HMS *Resolution*, forcing Cook to return to Kealakekua Bay to make repairs. On this occasion, the natives were much less friendly, and they stole the cutter of HMS *Discovery*. The following day, the 14th February 1779, Cook put ashore with nine marines to demand the return of the cutter. Without warning, warriors attacked the shore party with clubs, spears and knives killing Cook and four of the marines.

The natives removed Cook's body from the beach, and after preserving his hands in sea salt, they cut his body into pieces and stripped the flesh from the bones; the Hawaiian custom in the treatment of the remains of a high chief. According to tradition the owner of such bones inherited the spiritual power of the deceased. When peace resumed, the Hawaiians returned parts of Cook's body which included his skull and hands. The remains were placed in a casket and consigned to the waters of Kealakekua Bay on 21st February 1779.

Captain Cook Statue, West Cliff

Captain Cook's most famous ship was the *Endeavour*, which he used on his first voyage around the world. Previously called the *Earl of Pembroke*, the vessel was a Whitby cat, or collier, designed to transport coal from the north-east of England to London. After being refitted for the voyage, the Admiralty renamed and commissioned her as HM *Bark Endeavour*. The name 'Bark' identified her from another *Endeavour*, already in service at the time. The ship accommodated nearly one hundred officers and crew, marines and civilians, and it was the crew's main home during the three-year voyage.

For Cook's second voyage the Admiralty purchased two further Whitby colliers for conversion; the *Marquis of Granby* and the *Marquis of Rockingham*, renaming them HMS *Drake* and HMS *Raleigh*. However, the Secretary of State thought these names might offend the Spanish; subsequently they became HMS *Resolution* and HMS *Adventure*. The *Resolution* impressed Cook enough that he called her 'the ship of my choice' and 'a better ship for such service I never could wish for.' On his final voyage, Cook sailed again in the *Resolution* this time supported by HMS *Discovery*, yet another Whitby collier.

Robin Hood's Bay to Scarborough
SECTION EIGHT – 15 MILES (24.1KM)

Robin Hood's Bay

From Robin Hood's Bay, the Cleveland Way ascends to the windswept heights of Ravenscar 'the Town that never was,' and visits the hidden cove of Hayburn Wyke with its striking waterfalls. The trail undulates up and down like a roller-coaster dropping down through green valleys and wooded dells to sea level before rising back to the cliff tops, with excellent coastal scenery throughout.

The first written record for Robin Hood's Bay was in 1536 when King Henry VIII's topographer, John Leland, described it as 'a fisher townlet of twenty boats'. However, the origin of its name is unknown, and there is no evidence that Robin Hood of Sherwood Forest fame ever visited the bay. The name probably arose from a variety of legends and may refer to Robin (in the) Hood, an ancient forest sprite similar to Robin Goodfellow, a more familiar name used for comparable elves and fairies across the country. Apparently, he haunted the barrows on the moor above. Moreover, Robin Goodfellow was the alter-ego of Puck, that mischievous imp of English folklore, immortalised in William Shakespeare's play *A Midsummer Night's Dream*.

The village has always had a strong connection with the sea, although its thriving fishing fleet began to dwindle in the late nineteenth century and nowadays most of its income derives from tourism. However, during the eighteenth century, Robin Hood's Bay was reputedly the busiest smuggling port on the Yorkshire coast. The town's network of tiny streets supposedly has a labyrinth of underground passageways connecting the houses with each other. Evidently, the smuggled contraband could pass from the bay to the top of the village without leaving the cover of the houses.

Skirmishes between smugglers and excisemen frequently occurred, both at sea and on land, and smugglers' wives often poured boiling water over the excisemen as they passed through the narrow alleyways. Two excise cutters found themselves outgunned and were chased out of the bay in 1773 by three smuggling vessels. In 1779 a pitched battle took place in the bay over 200 kegs of brandy and gin, and fifteen sacks of tea – the smugglers won!

However, the excisemen were not the only threat to Bayfolk. In the late eighteenth and early nineteenth centuries, press gangs roamed the coastal villages searching for 'recruits'. Although fishermen were supposedly exempt from military service, this did not deter the press gangs; and once 'pressed', they were unlikely to return home for many years, if at all. The women of the village warned the menfolk by the beating of a drum when they saw the press gangs arriving in the bay; fierce battles followed to beat them off.

A plaque in the village records the details of a spectacular rescue 'On the 18th January 1881 the brig *Visitor* ran ashore at Robin Hood's Bay. No local boat could be launched on account of the violence of the storm, so the Whitby lifeboat was brought overland passing this point – a distance of 6 miles – through snowdrifts 7 feet deep on a road rising to 500 feet, with 200 men clearing the way ahead and with 18 horses heaving at the tow lines, whilst men worked uphill towards them from the bay. The lifeboat was launched two hours after leaving Whitby, and at the second attempt, the crew of the *Visitor* were saved.'

After leaving the bay, the trail follows the cliff top to Ravenscar dropping down to sea level on two occasions. The first leads to the beautiful inlet of Boggle Hole, another place associated with legends of hobgoblins. The local name for these mischievous sprites is 'boggle', and they supposedly lived in caves along the coast and the more secluded parts of the moors. Standing to the right of the trail is the Boggle Hole Youth Hostel, which was formerly a water-powered corn mill. Besides accommodation, the hostel has a dog-friendly café. The path returns briefly to the cliff top, before descending to cross the wooded ravine of Stoupe Beck.

Further along the cliff top, we pass the remains of a World War II pillbox; one of 28,000 such fortresses, built c.1940 as part of Britain's defence against the threat of Nazi invasion. There are glorious views of Robin Hood's Bay, which sweeps in a three-mile curve between the headlands from Ness Point to Old Peak, also known respectively as North Cheek and South Cheek. The Cleveland Way continues towards Ravenscar and passes through the site of the Peak Alum Works, where stone walls and foundations mark the position of the former buildings.

In the seventeenth century, the discovery of alum in the grey shale around Ravenscar transformed the coastal landscape into an industrial wasteland. Fifty tonnes of shale yielded one ton of alum, and left behind vast quarries and spoil heaps which are still visible on the hillside. The primary uses for alum were as a fixative for dyes and for softening leather during the tanning process. One of the critical ingredients used in its production was human urine! Most natural deodorants contain alum, which prevents the growth of bacteria and eliminates the odour related to sweat; fortunately, these products now utilise synthetic alum.

The Raven Hall Hotel, dating from 1774, was once a private residence owned by King George III's physician, Dr Francis Willis; there is a rumour that the King stayed at the hall for treatment during his bouts of madness.

Raven Hall Hotel, Ravenscar

Although the Willis family acquired great wealth, their son Rev. Dr Richard Willis soon squandered his inheritance through an addiction to gambling. According to one story, he lost the hall in a wager which involved two lice crawling across a plate!

From Ravenscar the trail returns to the cliff edge, passing the remains of the roads and kerbs laid down for 'the town that never was' *(see page 64)*. The path along the cliff top leads to the Ravenscar Radar Station, constructed in 1941 as part of the British early warning radar system. The station could reliably detect aircraft flying as low as 500 feet (150m) and remained in service until the end of World War II.

At Petard Point, we get our first glimpse of Scarborough Castle, and on a bright day, our final destination at Filey Brigg is visible. Further along the trail, we drop down steeply to reach the secluded cove of Hayburn Wyke where twin waterfalls cascade directly onto the boulder-strewn beach. The name is a combination of Hayburn, an Anglo-Saxon word meaning 'hunting enclosure by a stream' and Wyke which is the Norse word for 'sea inlet or creek'.

The densely wooded slopes are a haven for wildlife, with more than thirty species of breeding birds recorded, including blackcaps, spotted flycatchers, redstarts, willow warblers and woodpeckers, while badgers, foxes and roe deer frequent the forest fringes. In spring and early summer, wildflowers embellish the woodland with spectacular displays, clusters of wood anemone mingle in the yellow swathes of celandine, and then wild garlic compliments a carpet of bluebells, followed by other ground flora including lady's mantle and wild honeysuckle.

After regaining the cliff top at Roger Trod, Scarborough Castle reappears on the distant headland, and although it's still some six miles away, it dominates the view as we approach our goal for today. The trail leaves the National Park just before reaching the coastguard lookout station at Long Nab. From here the route remains reasonably level to Scalby Ness where we descend steeply to Scalby Mills.

The Cleveland Way continues along a level pedestrian promenade passing the Sea Life Centre and some colourful beach huts, with Scarborough Castle on the peninsula. Further along the road, there is a massive steel sculpture by the artist Ray Lonsdale. The figure, entitled *Freddie Gilroy and the Belsen Stragglers*, depicts Freddie Gilroy, a retired miner, who was one of the first soldiers to relieve the Bergen-Belsen concentration camp at the end of World War II.

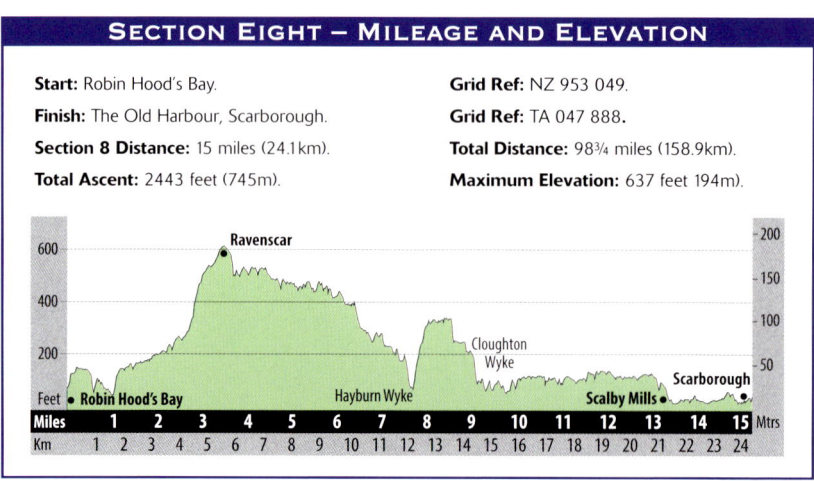

SECTION EIGHT – MILEAGE AND ELEVATION

Start: Robin Hood's Bay.
Finish: The Old Harbour, Scarborough.
Section 8 Distance: 15 miles (24.1km).
Total Ascent: 2443 feet (745m).

Grid Ref: NZ 953 049.
Grid Ref: TA 047 888.
Total Distance: 98¾ miles (158.9km).
Maximum Elevation: 637 feet 194m).

Map 24
Robin Hood's Bay to Ravenscar

① 953049 Leave Robin Hood's Bay by the side of the Smugglers Bistro *(SP Cleveland Way - Ravenscar 3m - England Coast Path)*. Follow the lane to Flagstaff Cottage, ascend some stone steps on the left *(SP Cleveland Way)* and then continue climbing via a wooden boardwalk.

② 952047 Join a stone-paved path and follow it along the top of the cliff.

③ 952045 Go through a gate *(SP Cleveland Way - Boggle Hole)*. Follow a fenced track and pass through another gate.

④ 954041 Descend steeply via some steps into the wooded ravine to the Boggle Hole Youth Hostel and café. Cross Mill Beck via the footbridge and ascend to the road.

⑤ 955040 Turn right and after a few yards leave the road via some steps on the left *(SP Cleveland Way - Ravenscar 2¾ mls)*. Ascend to the cliff top and continue to Stoupe Beck. Descend steeply back to sea level.

⑥ 958035 Cross the bridge *(SP Cleveland Way - Ravenscar)* bear right and follow a stepped path climbing back to the cliff top. Continue to the road at Stoupe Bank Farm. Turn left *(SP Cleveland Way - Ravenscar)* and follow the road for about 300 yards (275m).

⑦ 959031 Leave the road via a stile on the left *(SP Cleveland Way - Ravenscar)*, follow an enclosed path through a gate and continue to a WW2 pillbox. Now follow the cliff edge passing through a gate and crossing two footbridges. Continue along the track to a signpost.

⑧ 971022 Turn left *(SP Cleveland Way - Alum Works)*, cross a footbridge and go through a gate. Continue directly across the field and pass through another gate. Descend into the gully, cross a footbridge and ascend some steps. Follow the signposts around the alum works.

⑨ 974021 Leave the alum works at the south side *(Waymark)*. Follow an enclosed path to its end. Turn left *(SP Cleveland Way)* and continue on a broad farm track to a fork

⑩ 974018 Take the right fork *(SP Cleveland Way)* and ascend steeply on a narrow track. Turn left onto a broader track *(SP Cleveland Way)* climbing more gradually. At the next fork keep left *(SP Cleveland Way)*.

⑪ 979015 At the junction continue ahead on a concrete road, passing the National Trust Visitor Centre to reach the main road.

⑫ 980016 Route directions continue from **MAP 25 – POINT 12**.

63

Map 25
Ravenscar to Herbert Hole

12 **980016** Turn left and follow the road around onto Station Road *(SP Ravenscar)*. Continue over the brow of the road.

13 **981016** Leave the road via a rougher lane on the left *(SP Cleveland Way - Scarborough 11m)*. When the track narrows, continue straight ahead to a fence at the cliff edge.

14 **982019** Turn right *(Waymark)* and follow the path along the cliff top.

15 **986014** Continue ahead *(SP Cleveland Way)* and follow the path to the Ravenscar radar station situated in the field behind the coastguard station.

16 **992008** After passing the radar station go through a gate. At the next signpost *(SP Cleveland Way)* continue along the cliff path for about 2½ miles (4km) to reach a gate.

⚠ **004987** At the time of publication there was a temporary diversion in force from this point due to a landslip, see page 83.

17 **009979** Route directions continue from **MAP 26 – POINT 17**.

Refreshments, accommodation and toilets are available at Ravenscar.

RAVENSCAR
'THE TOWN THAT NEVER WAS'

In 1895 Victorian entrepreneurs made ambitious plans to turn Ravenscar into a luxurious holiday resort to rival Scarborough and Whitby. Their proposals included private houses, hotels, shops, formal gardens, promenade walks and a Marine Esplanade along the cliff top. The company immediately took on 300 workers to construct roads, lay mains drainage and mark out 1500 building plots. In 1900 a brickworks opened expecting to supply materials for the new town. Unfortunately, few people invested in the project and the company eventually went bankrupt in 1913 after which Ravenscar became famous as 'the town that never was'. However, the remains of the roads and kerbstones are still visible around the village.

MAP 26
HERBERT HOLE TO CROOK NESS

17 **009979** Go through the gate, and after a short descent, the path climbs over a ridge. Continue to a gate.

18 **010973** Pass through the gate and descend via wooden stairways and boardwalks to cross a footbridge. Climb back up slightly before descending a stone stepped path to cross a footbridge at Hayburn Wyke. **CAUTION: The descent is often slippery in places!**

19 **010971** To see the waterfalls turn left and descend a short distance to the beach. Afterwards return to the footbridge and ascend the stone-paved path. Turn left (SP Cleveland Way - Scarborough 5½m) and follow the waymarks and signposts through the wood.

20 **009968** Turn left (SP Cleveland Way - Scarborough 5½m), and ascend from the wood, now follow the cliff top to a bench seat.

21 **017961** Bear left and follow the cliff path (SP Cleveland Way) to a wooded ravine.

22 **020957** Descend steeply and cross the ravine. Continue along the cliff path and cross over the small ravine at Salt Pans.

23 **020952** Bear left and ascend some steps. At a waymark/SP bear left and descend to cross Cloughton Wyke. Climb some steps leading back to the cliff top.

24 **019950** At a three-way marker post keep left and continue across two more ravines to reach the Long Nab Coastguard Station. Follow the path towards Crook Ness.

25 **027935** Route directions continue from **MAP 27 – POINT 25**.

Refreshments, accommodation and toilets are available at the Hayburn Wyke Inn.

DETOUR TO VISIT THE HAYBURN WYKE INN

A **010971** After visiting the waterfalls, ascend the paved path. Bear right at a fork (SP Hayburn Wyke Inn ¼m) and climb through the wood to a gate.

B **007971** Go through the gate, bear left and continue to the inn. From the inn, follow a rough track on the left and go through a gate. Bear left and pass through a gate leading back into the wood.

C **009968** Turn right (SP Cleveland Way) and ascend from the wood, now follow the cliff top to a bench seat. Directions continue from **POINT 21**.

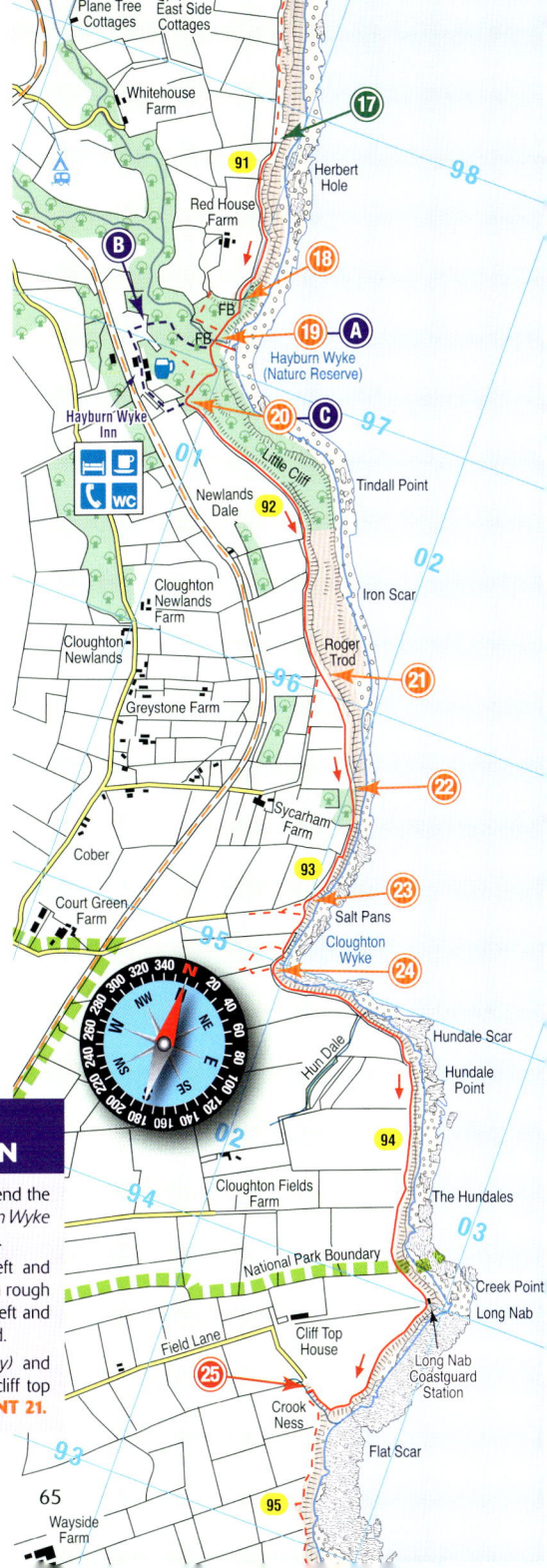

65

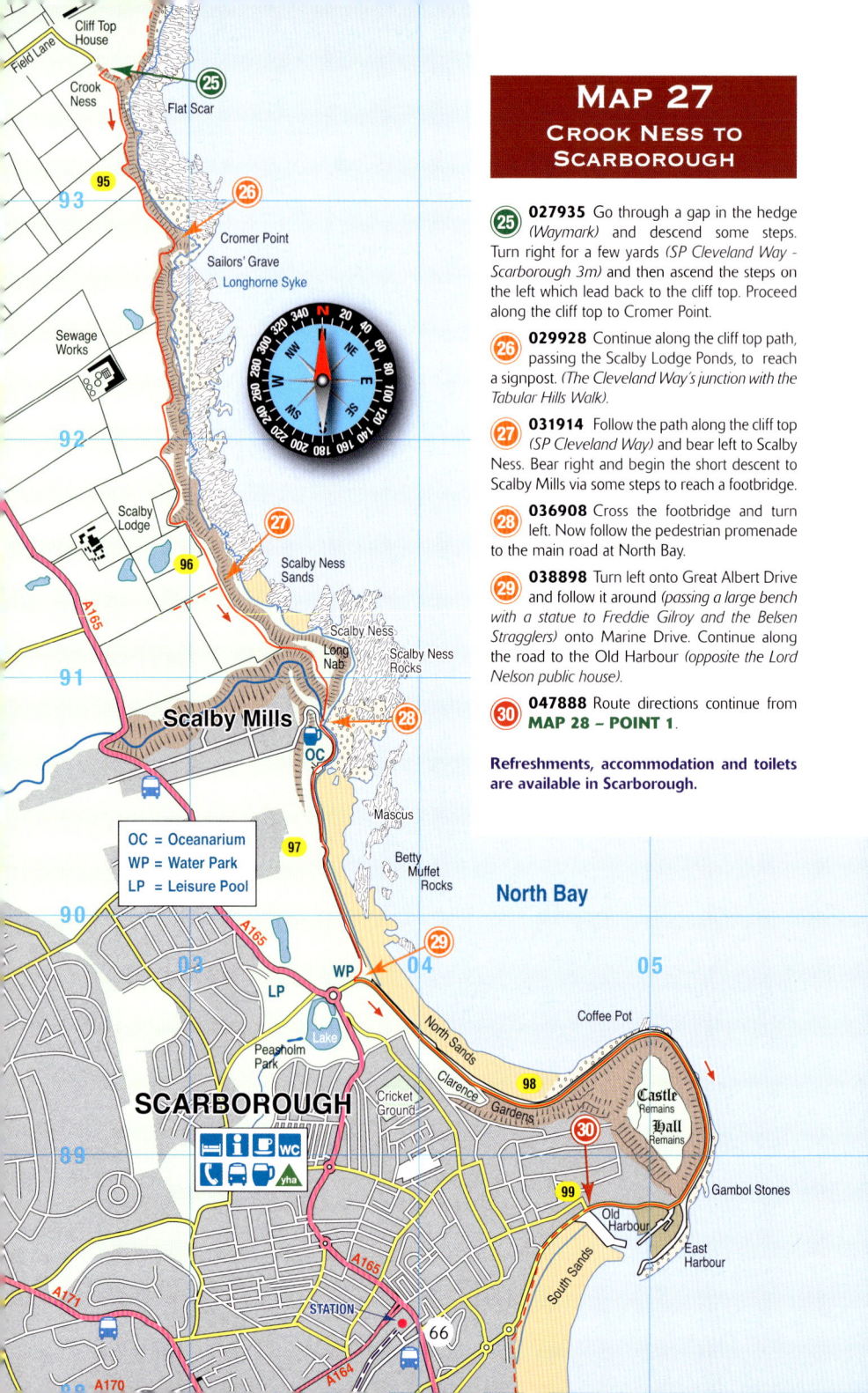

MAP 27
CROOK NESS TO SCARBOROUGH

027935 Go through a gap in the hedge *(Waymark)* and descend some steps. Turn right for a few yards *(SP Cleveland Way - Scarborough 3m)* and then ascend the steps on the left which lead back to the cliff top. Proceed along the cliff top to Cromer Point.

029928 Continue along the cliff top path, passing the Scalby Lodge Ponds, to reach a signpost. *(The Cleveland Way's junction with the Tabular Hills Walk).*

031914 Follow the path along the cliff top *(SP Cleveland Way)* and bear left to Scalby Ness. Bear right and begin the short descent to Scalby Mills via some steps to reach a footbridge.

036908 Cross the footbridge and turn left. Now follow the pedestrian promenade to the main road at North Bay.

038898 Turn left onto Great Albert Drive and follow it around *(passing a large bench with a statue to Freddie Gilroy and the Belsen Stragglers)* onto Marine Drive. Continue along the road to the Old Harbour *(opposite the Lord Nelson public house).*

047888 Route directions continue from **MAP 28 – POINT 1**.

Refreshments, accommodation and toilets are available in Scarborough.

Scarborough

BRITAIN'S FIRST SEASIDE RESORT

Castle Hill, Scarborough

Scarborough's most dominant feature is the high craggy peninsula of **Castle Hill** which juts out into the North Sea and separates the seafront into two beautiful sandy bays. The ruins of Scarborough Castle crown the summit, where an Iron Age fortification and a Roman signal station previously stood.

The origin of the town's name is intriguing. According to the Scandinavian *Kormáks saga*, the brothers Thorgils and Kormak went harrying in Ireland, Wales, England and Scotland and established the stronghold called Skarthaborg in AD 966. Evidently, the name derives from Thorgils' nickname 'Skarthi' which is the Old Norse word for 'hare-lip' and 'borg' meaning 'fortified place'.

In September 1066 Harald Hardrada, King of Norway, invaded England and raided the east coast, burning Scarborough to the ground. However, his conquest was brief as Harold II, King of England, met the invasion force at Stamford Bridge on 25th September 1066 and defeated the invaders, slaughtering many of them and killing Hardrada. Apparently, the Norwegian losses were so severe that they only needed twenty-four ships from the invasion fleet of 300 to carry the survivors home.

The castle, which dates from 1138, has suffered sieges from medieval kings and Civil War armies. From the 1650s Scarborough Castle served as a prison; in 1665 George Fox, the founder of the Quakers, was one of the inmates. Furthermore, in December 1914, during the opening months of World War I, German battleships entered the bay and bombarded the town and castle, killing eighteen civilians and severely wounding many others. After the attack, Scarborough became part of the government's recruitment campaign. One poster just stated: 'Avenge Scarborough - up and at 'em now!'

In 1626 Elizabeth Farrer, the wife of one of Scarborough's leading citizens, discovered a natural spring where the Spa Complex now stands. The waters tasted slightly acidic, and she believed that they had medicinal qualities and could cure an abundance of minor ailments. Thus Scarborough Spa was born, Britain's first seaside resort attracting thousands of visitors to the town, which became known as the 'Queen of Watering Places'. However, the 'taking of the waters' ceased in the late 1960s with the water being declared unfit for consumption. Nevertheless, the Spa Complex continues to provide entertainment and is a venue for conferences, exhibitions, live music and other events. Moreover, a Victorian cliff tramway links the Spa Complex with the South Cliff, which rises 200 feet (60m) above the bay.

Scarborough to Filey

SECTION NINE – 10 MILES (16.1 KM)

The concluding part of the Cleveland Way leaves the hustle and bustle of Scarborough behind and returns us to the more enjoyable cliff paths. The coastal scenery is stunning, and with just ten miles remaining, we can reflect on some of the most memorable experiences of our journey.

Resuming from the harbour, we continue along the seafront around the South Bay passing the Spa Complex. As the path begins to ascend away from the shoreline, we pass below the former site of the Holbeck Hall Hotel. In June 1993 the hotel became the focus of the global media when a landslip left the building hovering perilously close to the cliff edge. The landslide continued its path of destruction for another two days, after which the hotel finally succumbed to the crumbling cliff and slipped into the sea. According to the British Geological Survey, the slide caused about one million tonnes of silty clay to fall into the sea, creating a semicircular promontory 650 feet (200m) in width and projecting 440 feet (135m) outwards from the foot of the cliff. Consolidation and landscaping of the area have left little evidence of the dramatic end of the ill-fated hotel.

The walk continues beside the South Cliff Golf Course and follows a clear path to Osgodby, and after a brief road walk, we descend through woodland to the beautiful expanse of Cayton Bay. The beach is quiet and unspoilt, comprising a long sweep of fine sand, and is popular with surfers and windsurfers.

During World War II, Cayton Bay was a 'dangerous beach', i.e. regarded as a possible location for enemy invasion. One of the primary concerns was that Nazi forces would land in the bay, scale the cliffs and join airborne troops to form a bridgehead which would enable them to attack the port of Scarborough from the rear. However, British anti-invasion preparations included the construction of reinforced concrete pillboxes and anti-tank cubes along the coastline in vulnerable places such as Cayton Bay to make the country an impregnable fortress. The remains of these are visible along the beach, and a former section post overlooks the bay from Killerby Cliff, although this is now projecting precariously over the edge of the cliff as a result of coastal erosion.

After rising gradually to Lebberston Cliff, the route passes close to the burial site of a Bronze Age warrior, known today as the 'Gristhorpe Man'. In July 1834, landowner

Scarborough Lighthouse

William Beswick excavated a barrow on the cliffs near Gristhorpe, which now lies within the area of the Blue Dolphin Holiday Park. The dig unearthed an intact log coffin, fashioned from the hollowed-out trunk of a large oak tree, which contained a well-preserved skeleton stained black from the oak tannins.

Further examination by the University of Bradford in 2005 revealed that 'Gristhorpe Man' was around six feet (1.82m) in height and about 60 years old when he died c.4000 years ago. The Bradford team concluded that he was a high-status individual, possibly a tribal chieftain and judging by his stature had a relatively healthy diet. Other evidence of his social standing comes from the artefacts buried with him. These included a bronze dagger with a whalebone pommel, flint tools and a wicker basket containing food residue. Although his skeleton has several healed fractures consistent with the life of a warrior, evidently he died from natural causes. The remains of 'Gristhorpe Man' are on display in the Rotunda Museum in Scarborough.

At Cunstone Nab the final goal of this long trek is now within our grasp. During the last few miles to Filey, the views extend beyond the Brigg to the towering chalk cliffs of Bempton and Flamborough Head. As we approach Filey, a sizeable stone marker celebrates the official end of the Cleveland

Donkey's taking a break

Way near Filey Brigg. Moreover, the marker also commemorates the Yorkshire Wolds Way, which stretches 79 miles (127km) to (or from) Hessle on the banks of the mighty Humber estuary.

Before heading into Filey, continue along the grassy cliff path leading onto the headland to enjoy views from the most easterly point of the route. Please do not attempt to descend from the cliff top to reach the Brigg, the cliffs are dangerous. However, if the tide is receding, it is possible to walk along Filey Sands to Brigg End. Afterwards, return along the sands and enjoy the delights of Filey. Well, that's it, 'The End' of the Cleveland Way, I hope you take away fond memories of this inspiring journey.

SECTION NINE – MILEAGE AND ELEVATION

Start: The Old Harbour, Scarborough.
Finish: Filey bus station.
Section 9 Distance: 10 miles (16.1km).
Total Ascent: 1806 feet (550m).

Grid Ref: TA 047 888.
Grid Ref: TA 115 807.
Total Distance: 109 miles (175km)
Maximum Elevation: 325 feet (99m).

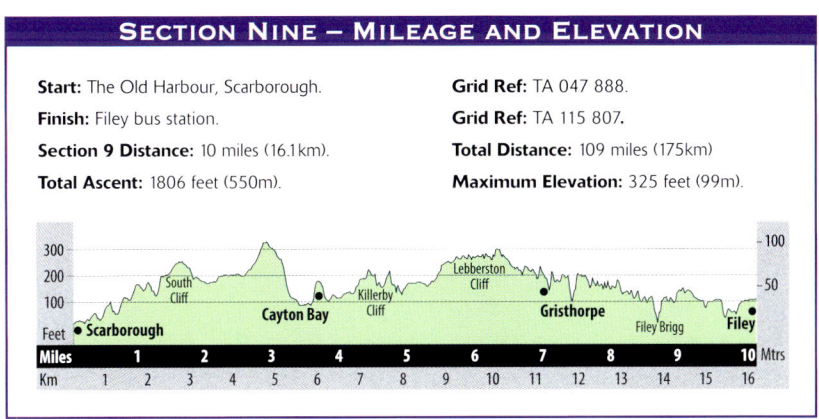

MAP 28
SCARBOROUGH TO CAYTON BAY

① **047888** From the old harbour, continue along the seafront to a roundabout.

② **044882** Turn left and follow the road to the Spa Pavilion. After passing the pavilion go through an underpass to reach the Cliff Lifts. Continue to some beach huts.

③ **045877** Bear left and follow the seawall to its end.

④ **048873** Continue ahead on a rough track and begin ascending to the cliff top.

⑤ **050870** Turn right *(SP Filey 8 miles)* and continue ascending. At the first junction, keep left and follow a narrow path to a signpost *(SP Filey 7½ miles)*. Continue along the cliff top.

⑥ **058863** Descend into a ravine, turn right onto a broad track *(SP Cleveland Way)* and ascend to a signpost.

⑦ **057861** Turn left *(SP Cleveland Way)* and follow a narrow path, cross a wooden bridge and continue along the cliff top. Turn right *(SP Cleveland Way)* and follow an enclosed path to the main road.

⑧ **058852** Turn left *(SP Cleveland Way - Filey)* and follow the road to its end.

⑨ **061849** Go through a gap on the left *(SP Acorn) (Cayton Bay NT)* and descend a stepped path. Turn right *(SP Acorn)* and follow the track to descend a few more steps.

⑩ **063849** Continue along the cliff edge, descend some steps and go through a gate. Turn left and follow the path to a fence.

⑪ **066845** Route directions continue from **MAP 29 – POINT 11**.

HIGH TIDES ROUTE

During heavy seas, it may be necessary to use an alternative route from point 3.

Ⓐ **045877** Bear right and pass behind some beach huts to reach the Clock Cafe. Ascend a winding path to reach the Esplanade near the Holbeck Clock Tower. *(Or you could take the cliff lift if its open).*

Ⓑ **046871** Turn left along the Esplanade and continue to a T-junction. Turn left into Holbeck Hill and then turn left into Sea Cliff Road.

Ⓒ **049869** Turn right and pass through the car park. Descend on a broad track, turn right and continue along the cliff top to **POINT 6**.

MAP 29
CAYTON BAY TO NEWBIGGIN CLIFF

11 **066845** Turn right and go through a gate. Continue along a stepped path ascending to a signpost, *(SP Cleveland Way)* go through a gate on the left and descend to the narrow service road for the pumping station.

12 **067843** Cross the road *(SP Cleveland Way)* and climb the steps opposite to return to the cliff top, continue to Killerby Cliff.

13 **069842** Bear left *(SP Cleveland Way) - Filey 5 miles)* and follow a clear path leading around Leberston Cliff to Red Cliff Point.

14 **083841** After descending from Red Cliff Point the trail climbs gradually towards the caravan sites on the hill top. Follow a gravel road passing in front of the static caravans.

15 **090835** When the gravel road sweeps right, bear left *(SP Cleveland Way)* pass beside some more static caravans, climbing slightly. Go through a gap in the hedge and continue on a narrow path around the perimeter of the caravan parks.

16 **099828** After passing the last of the holiday parks the trail continues around The Wyke and along Newbiggin Cliff.

17 **107825** Route directions continue from **MAP 30 – POINT 17**.

ARE YOU GOING TO SCARBOROUGH FAIR?

In the Middle Ages, Scarborough Fair was internationally famous and attracted merchants from all over England and Europe, and as far away as the Byzantine Empire. Minstrels, dancers, jugglers and fortune tellers came to entertain the crowds of buyers, sellers and pleasure-seekers. The fair continued to take place for over 500 years, subsequently closing in 1788 due to competition from rival towns. Moreover, *Scarborough Fair* is also a traditional English folk song. The lyrics inspired the pop duo, Simon and Garfunkel, to use the ballad in the soundtrack for the 1967 film *The Graduate*, starring Anne Bancroft and Dustin Hoffman.

Map 30
Newbiggin Cliff to North Cliff

The official end of the Cleveland Way

(17) 107825 From Newbiggin Cliff the route follows a broad grassy track leading to the stone marker which indicates the end of the Cleveland Way. However, the marker is about 1¾ miles (2.8km) from Filey town centre, which is the most practical finish for our journey.

(18) 125817 From the marker the route follows the Wolds Way. Bear left along a narrow track leading onto Filey Brigg.

(19) 130815 Retrace your steps from the brigg, turn left and follow the cliff edge. Cross a ravine via a stepped path and continue to another stepped path leading down to the main road. Turn left and descend to reach Beach Road at Cobble Landing.

(20) 120808 To reach the bus station continue along Beach Road. Turn right onto Cargate Hill. Continue onto Murray Street and Station Avenue. Near the top of Station Avenue turn left into the bus station. **THE END**.

Filey

THE EAST RIDING OF YORKSHIRE

Since Victorian times, Filey has been one of the North's most popular seaside resorts where holidaymakers can enjoy beautiful sands which are both safe and clean. Its long crescent-shaped beach extends south from Filey Brigg to the start of Bempton Cliffs, a distance of about 6 miles (10km).

Filey's entry in Domesday Book is 'Fiuelac,' thought to mean 'the five leys,' 'ley' being the Anglo-Saxon word for a clearing. However, it was the Romans who first recognised the importance of Filey. In the fourth century AD, they established a signal station on the narrow peninsula at Carr Naze to warn of invasion by sea-borne raiders from across the North Sea. Moreover, the rocky Spittal below, running out from the Brigg, most likely served as a natural harbour for Roman sailing vessels.

In addition to being an impressive landmark, Filey Brigg is a haven for both naturalists and geologists, it provides a natural environment for marine life, and its copious rock pools are popular attractions. One of the more significant pools, known as the Emperor's Bath, takes its name from Emperor Constantine, who, according to tradition, bathed in the pool while visiting this remote part of his empire. The rocks and the intertidal region attract many species of birds, including oystercatchers, purple sandpipers and redshanks which visit the shoreline throughout the winter months.

The oldest building in Filey is St Oswald's Parish Church, founded c.1180 by the Augustinian Friars from Bridlington Priory. The church consists of a nave, north and south transepts, chancel and a west gallery. Its embattled square tower houses three bells and a large gilded fish serves as a weathervane. Sir Nikolaus Pevsner, the architectural historian, in his description of St Oswald's wrote, 'This is easily the finest

Fisherman sculpture, Cobble Landing

church in the NE corner of the East Riding'. The church stands on the northern brow of a ravine, which was the boundary between the North and East Ridings of Yorkshire until 1888. Therefore, St Oswald's was in the North Riding, and its congregation resided in the East Riding.

In 1939 Filey Holiday Camp was being built for Billy Butlin. However, following the outbreak of the World War II, an agreement with the War Ministry funded the resort's completion. The ministry requisitioned the camp to use as a military training base known as RAF Hunmanby Moor. When the war ended in 1945, Butlin reclaimed the site, which became a popular holiday resort and played a significant part in Filey's economy for more than forty years. At its peak, Butlin's Filey Camp was catering for almost 11,000-holidaymakers. Nevertheless, it became increasingly difficult to fill the camp with sufficient numbers for profitability, and it closed in 1983.

Places near the Cleveland Way

TOWNS AND VILLAGES CLOSE TO THE TRAIL

The following towns and villages are not on the actual route of the Cleveland Way. However, they are within reach and may assist with the planning of your journey. The shortest walking distances from the trail are for one way only.

Abbreviations: 🍺 *pub;* ☕ *cafe;* 🚾 *toilets;* 🛏 *accommodation;* 📞 *telephone;* *CW - Cleveland Way - distance from.*

SECTION 1

Scawton – In medieval times the road through the village was the main highway, constructed by the monks to provide a quick route between the monasteries of Byland and Rievaulx. According to tradition the monks also built the Hare Inn during the twelfth century to refresh travellers on this ancient road, although much of the inn's present structure dates from the eighteenth century.
CW ½ mile (800m). 🍺 📞

Old Byland, as the name implies, is close to a site formerly chosen by the monks of Byland Abbey in 1143. However, its proximity to Rievaulx, already well established, caused much distress to both monasteries. Each abbey could hear the other's bells at all hours of day and night, this was 'not fitting and could by no means be endured'. As the later arrivals, the Byland monks gave way, and in 1147 they moved to another temporary site at Oldstead. The church, dedicated to All Saints, has some very interesting Norman and Saxon fragments.
CW 1½ miles (2.4km).

SECTION 2

Boltby nestles in a valley at the foot of the Hambleton Hills on the border of the North York Moors National Park. The village is Danish in origin, and its name means 'Bolt's farm'. At the time of the Domesday Survey, Boltby was the property of Hugh, the son of Baldric. Later the village fell into the possession of a family who took their surname from it. One owner was Odo de Boltby, who gave land and was a benefactor to the Preceptory of Mount St John. Moreover, he built a castle in the valley, near the road leading over Hambleton, sited on the farm called Low Paradise.
CW 1 mile (1.6km). ☕ 📞 🛏

Kepwick's entry in Domesday Book is 'Chipuic'. The present spelling is Scandinavian in origin, and derives from Kaeplinge meaning 'Kæppi's vik' or 'nook in the hills'. The village has a private memorial chapel, built in 1894. The west window depicts St Michael and some of the more heroic biblical characters and saints. The east window, designed by Clayton and Bell after World War I, shows the Resurrection.
CW 2 miles (3.2km). 📞

Nether and **Over Silton** sit on the edge of the National Park, about one mile apart. All Saints Church at Nether Silton has a Norman tub font adorned with a bold cable moulding. The altar rails have twisted balusters, reputedly made from the wood of HMS *Dreadnought* which participated in the Battle of Trafalgar in 1805. Over Silton's church, dedicated to St Mary, dates back to at least the twelfth century, although it occupies an older Saxon religious site. The fourteenth-century bellcote houses an ancient bell, inscribed 'Ave Maria Gracia Plena' said to have come from Mount Grace Priory.
CW 2 miles (3.2km). 🍺 📞

SECTION 3

Swainby is an attractive, peaceful village situated along the banks of a tree-shaded stream. The name derives from the old Norse 'sveinn', meaning 'Swain's farm'. Although a

small settlement existed here in the thirteenth century, it only achieved significance with the arrival of the plague – the Black Death – when nearby Whorlton succumbed. The survivors deserted their village and moved to Swainby shortly after the outbreak was over.
CW 1 mile (1.6km).

Faceby is a picturesque hamlet which derives its name from the Old Norse meaning 'Feit's farm'. It has a pub, village hall and an enchanting church dedicated to St Mary Magdalene. The present structure, rebuilt in 1875, incorporates some fragments from the original twelfth-century building.
CW 1¼ miles (2km).

Carlton-in-Cleveland is a charming village tucked away at the foot of the Cleveland Hills. Its pub, the Blackwell Ox, takes its name from a weighty shorthorn bull bred near Darlington. There is a story told of George Sangar, the vicar, who arrived here in the nineteenth century to find the church derelict. Without any funds he set about restoring the building himself, toiling day and night to provide the village with a place where they could worship with dignity. Unfortunately, shortly after its completion in 1881, a fire broke out and destroyed it. The present church, dedicated to St Botolph, was built in 1897.
CW 1½ miles (2.4km).

SECTION 4

Great Broughton – the name 'Broughton' means 'farmstead by a brook', and 'Great' distinguishes it from the adjacent hamlet of Little Broughton. Their entries in Domesday Book are 'Magna Broctun' and 'Parva Broctun'.
CW 2 miles (3.2km).

Chop Gate has a chapel, school, village hall and a cosy pub - the Buck Inn. The village is known locally as Chop Yat for which the rough translation is 'pedlars' way', from 'ceap' the old English term for a pedlar or chapman, and 'yat' a dialect word for 'gate' or 'pass'. The name possibly arose in medieval times when pedlars toured the countryside. They also visited remote farms and villages selling merchandise to those who had difficulty in travelling to the market towns.
CW 2 miles (3.2km).

Ingleby Greenhow sits at the foot of a dramatic valley, sheltered by the steep Cleveland escarpment. Its entry in Domesday Book is 'Engleby', meaning 'village of the English', and the addition of Greenhow, which means 'the green hill', distinguishes it from two other Inglebys in the district.
CW 2 mile (3.2km).

SECTION 5

Great Ayton was the boyhood home of Captain James Cook, the British navigator and explorer, who rose from humble beginnings to become the most legendary seaman of his time. Cook attended the Postgate School, which now serves as the Captain Cook Schoolroom Museum.
CW 2 miles (3.2km).

Newton-under-Roseberry – Newton translates to 'new town', and 'under-Roseberry' distinguishes it from other places with a similar name. St Oswald's Church is a small, ancient structure, consisting of a Norman nave and chancel arch. In 1901 Temple Moore added the tower. An Anglo-Saxon stone carving set into the south-east buttress of the tower depicts a dragon attacking a quadruped. The church was formerly subordinate to Ayton and controlled by the monks of Whitby Abbey.
CW 1 mile (1.6km).

Guisborough is an ancient market town and its market cross, embellished by a sundial, stands at the head of the main street. Standing behind the Parish Church of St Nicholas are the ruins of Gisborough Priory, founded *c.*1119 by the local Bruce family, ancestors of Robert the Bruce, King

of Scotland. The Priory became one of the wealthiest houses in the North and also one of the most magnificent. The dramatic skeleton of the priory church's east end dominates the ruins and provides a glimpse of the monastery's former glory.
CW ¾ mile (1.2km).

Hutton Village initially called Thomas Town after Henry Thomas, the first landowner who built the village in the 1850s, to house workers from his ironstone mines at Cod Hill. Sir Joseph Whitwell Pease bought the estate in the 1860s and renamed it Hutton in 1880.
CW ¾ mile (1.2km).

Section 6

Brotton's entry in Domesday Book is 'Broctune' which means, 'farmstead by a brook'. Its population increased significantly in the nineteenth century after the discovery of ironstone. Lumpsey Mine, the largest of the Brotton mines, opened in the 1880s and closed in 1954. During World War I a rail-mounted artillery piece defended the mine against Zeppelin attack.
CW 1 mile (1.6km).

Loftus derives its name from the Old Norse 'lopt' meaning 'loft' and 'hus' meaning 'house' or simply 'house(s) with a loft'. The village dates back to at least the seventh century, and nearby excavations revealed an Anglo-Saxon cemetery. Finds included a rare bed burial in which a female body is laid out on a decorated wooden bed adorned with beautiful gold jewellery.
CW 1 mile (1.6km).

Hinderwell apparently takes its name from 'Hild's well', a holy well in the grounds of St Hilda's Church. According to tradition, while returning to Whitby Abbey, St Hilda stopped here, and after praying for water a spring appeared. St Hilda's Well became a pilgrimage site for monks travelling between the religious houses of Kirkham and Whitby.
CW 1 mile (1.6km).

Section 7

Lythe, located on the top of a long, steep hill, takes its name from the Scandinavian word 'hlith' meaning 'slope'. An ancient custom of 'Firing the Stiddy' exists to signal notable events. The Stiddy is an upturned anvil originally placed outside the blacksmith's shop. After filling the base with gunpowder, the charge is detonated by the heated tip of a long iron bar, and a loud explosion follows.
CW 1 mile (1.6km).

Hawsker consists of two parts, known as High and Low, and it initially had a cobbler, tailor, blacksmith and a windmill. Of these only the mill at Low Hawsker remains. Further along the road is the shaft of Hawsker Cross, which is an excellent example of a tenth-century Anglo-Saxon wayside cross. The cross comprises a stone base, split into two halves near the socket hole, and a shaft broken off just below the head.
CW 1½ miles (2.4km).

Section 8

Cloughton, pronounced Cloh-tun, is situated less than a mile from the sea. Although a small village, its facilities are excellent and include a church, pub, tea shop, general store and also a regular bus service. St Mary's Church contains a marble tablet in memory of William Bower and his wife Priscilla, dated 1704, which records that William and Priscilla lived long and comfortably in wedlock for 73 years. The inscription includes: 'They live well who love well, They die well who live well'.
CW ¾ mile (1.2km).

Burniston is the last village before reaching the built-up areas of Scalby Mills and Scarborough. Amenities include a village hall, which it shares with neighbouring Cloughton, two public houses, two churches and a Post Office.
CW 1½ miles (2.4km).

Equipment

WHAT TO TAKE WITH YOU

Walkers with experience of long-distance routes will no doubt have personal preferences on the equipment needed. However, anyone undertaking a long trail for the first time may find the information here helpful.

What to wear and carry with you will depend on the season, the weather and simple common sense. Moreover, provided you have the necessary equipment, your journey along the trail will not only be much safer but also more enjoyable.

When selecting equipment always visit a specialist outdoor shop first, ask for advice, the staff are often enthusiasts themselves. Try on boots, rucksacks and clothing for size and comfort. Then, if you decide to buy the same brand of items elsewhere or online, the measurements should be correct.

Shell clothing is vital to shield you from the elements. The choice is vast; the more expensive breathable garments double as windproofs and also help to reduce the condensation problems associated with cheaper nylon garments. Sturdy, comfortable walking boots are essential for ankle support, especially on steep descents and across uneven ground. Always 'break in' new boots before undertaking long-distance trails such as the Cleveland Way. Another essential item is a well-fitting rucksack to carry all of your equipment. Adjust the rucksack straps so that your shoulders carry the load, supported by the back and legs and other muscles, enabling you to maintain an upright posture.

Furthermore, consider using some walking poles, which will help to reduce the compressive force on your joints by up to twenty-five per cent. They will also improve your balance and provide a feeling of security and confidence, particularly during downhill descents and on slippery surfaces such as mud, snow, and loose rock.

The following lists are only suggestions, therefore, consider carefully what your personal needs are. Nevertheless, due to our unpredictable climate, a spare wool sweater and waterproofs are always advisable.

TO WEAR

Sturdy walking boots or stout shoes
Woollen socks
Cotton shirt or T-Shirt
Walking breeches, trousers or shorts
Woollen hat, balaclava or sun hat

TO CARRY

A small rucksack in which to carry the following items:
Anorak or cagoule
Overtrousers, gaiters
Fleece or woollen sweater
Gloves, scarf
Compass, whistle
First aid kit, antiseptic wipes
Tick removal tool
Ordnance Survey maps of the area
Torch, pencil and notepad
Emergency rations, survival bag
Water bottle with water
Food and snacks
High visibility vest *(to wear in poor light and during the shooting season on grouse moors)*

OPTIONAL ITEMS

Binoculars
Camera and spare films or memory card
Flask with tea, coffee, soup or other hot beverage
GPS
Swiss army knife
Walking poles

Accommodation and Planning

Useful Addresses

Planning a long distance walk yourself can be quite daunting. Fortunately, there are now many companies which can assist with the booking of your accommodation. Some of these will also arrange to transfer your luggage between each of your overnight stops.

The first decision to make is the number of days you wish to take for the completion of the trail. Build in several rest days to allow you to explore the towns and villages en route. The advantage of using a baggage transfer service means that you can pack as much as you require. Moreover, a lighter rucksack will make your walk much more pleasurable.

Booking Services

The companies in the following list provide accommodation booking services. Inclusion in this list does not imply any endorsement.

AbsoluteEscapes
Web: www.absoluteescapes.com

Book My Trail
Web: www.bookmytrail.com

Brigantes
Web: www.brigantesenglishwalks.com

Celtic Trails
Web: www.celtictrailswalkingholidays.co.uk

Contours Walking Holidays
Web: www.contours.co.uk

Discovery Travel
Web: www.discoverytravel.co.uk

Freedom Walking Holidays
Web: www.freedomwalkingholidays.co.uk

HF Holidays
Web: www.hfholidays.co.uk

Macs Adventure
Web: www.macsadventure.com

Mickledore Travel
Web: www.mickledore.co.uk

Shepherds Walks Holidays
Web: www.shepherdswalksholidays.co.uk

Sherpa Van Project
Web: www.sherpavan.com

The Walking Holiday Company
Web: www.thewalkingholidaycompany.co.uk

Wandering Aengus Treks
Web: www.watreks.com

Weather Goat Walk Support
Web: www.weathergoatwalks.co.uk

Where to walk
Web: www.where2walk.co.uk

Youth Hostels

The Youth Hostels Association (YHA) has five Youth Hostels along the Cleveland Way. Full details of the hostels below are available from YHA, Trevelyan House, Dimple Road, Matlock, Derbyshire, DE4 3XA.
☎ 01629 592700. Web: www.yha.org.uk

Helmsley Youth Hostel
Carlton Lane, Helmsley,
North Yorkshire, YO62 5HB
☎ 0845 371 9638.

Osmotherley Youth Hostel
Cote Ghyll Mill, Osmotherley, Northallerton,
North Yorkshire, DL6 3AH
☎ 0845 371 9035.

Whitby Youth Hostel
Abbey House, East Cliff, Whitby,
North Yorkshire YO22 4JT
☎ 0845 371 9049.

Boggle Hole Youth Hostel
Mill Beck, Fylingthorpe, Whitby,
North Yorkshire, YO22 4UQ
☎ 0845 371 9504.

Scarborough Youth Hostel
The White House, Burniston Road,
Scarborough, North Yorkshire, YO13 0DA
☎ 0845 371 9657.

INFORMATION CENTRES

Further details for accommodation, camping, transport and leisure services are available from Tourist Information Centres (TICs) and National Trails www.nationaltrail.co.uk/cleveland-way produce an online guide.

Filey TIC
John Street, Filey,
North Yorkshire, YO14 9DW.
☎ 01723 383636.

Great Ayton TIC
High Green Car Park, Great Ayton, TS9 6BJ.
☎ 01642 722835.

Guisborough TIC
Priory Grounds, Church Street
Guisborough, TS14 6HG.
☎ 01287 633801.

Helmsley TIC
Helmsley Castle, Castlegate,
Helmsley, North Yorkshire, YO62 5AB.
☎ 01439 770173.

Ravenscar National Trust Coastal Centre
Ravenscar, Scarborough,
North Yorkshire, YO13 0NE.
☎ 01723 870138/870423.

Robin Hood's Bay
The Old Coastguard Station.
☎ 01947 885900.

Saltburn TIC
Saltburn Library, Windsor Road
Saltburn, TS12 1AT
☎ 01287 622422.

Scarborough TIC
Harbourside, Sandside, Scarborough,
North Yorkshire, YO11 1PP.
☎ 01723 383636.

Sutton Bank National Park Visitor Centre
Sutton Bank, Thirsk,
North Yorkshire, YO7 2EH.
☎ 01845 597426.

Staithes Gateway Centre
Whitegate Close, Staithes, TS13 5BB.
☎ 01947 844100.

Thirsk TIC
49 Market Place, Thirsk,
North Yorkshire, YO7 1HA.
☎ 01845 522755.

Whitby TIC
Langbourn Road, Whitby,
North Yorkshire, YO21 1YN.
☎ 01723 383636.

Lyme Disease

SYMPTOMS, TREATMENT AND RISK REDUCTION

Walking is an enjoyable and healthy activity, and providing you follow a few simple rules it's also quite safe. Although most people take extra care as they walk along narrow country lanes, many are unaware that one of the most significant health threats to walkers is Lyme disease, a bacterial infection, which spreads to humans through the bite of an infected sheep tick.

Ticks are tiny bloodsucking, arachnids which live in areas of dense vegetation, such as bracken, long grass or woodlands. These minute creatures attach themselves to the skin of both animals and humans to feed on their blood. The life cycle of a tick takes two years and has four stages: egg, larva, nymph and adult. During this period, ticks will feed on three separate hosts. The larval tick feeds on the first host for several days; then it falls off and metamorphoses into a nymph. The nymphs remain inactive until the following spring when they find host number two; after feeding, they drop off and transform into adult ticks. The adults find their third host, feed on its blood and then mate. After feeding the ticks drop off, the male dies, but the female lives through the winter and lays approximately 3000 eggs the following spring – completing the cycle.

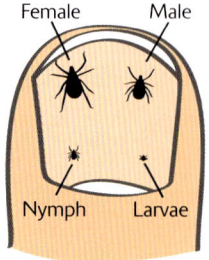

Symptoms. – During the early stages of Lyme disease, many people develop a red, circular skin rash known as *erythema migrans*. The rash, which may be diffuse and hard to discern, may not always appear at the bite site, but elsewhere and can develop up to thirty days after being bitten. However, about one in three people infected with Lyme disease do not see a rash. Some people also have flu-like symptoms in the early stages, such as a high temperature, or feeling hot and shivery, headaches, muscle and joint pain, tiredness and loss of energy.

Not all tick bites cause Lyme disease. Only ticks infected with the bacteria can cause Lyme disease in humans. Nevertheless, it's still important to be aware of ticks and remove them safely as soon as possible just in case.

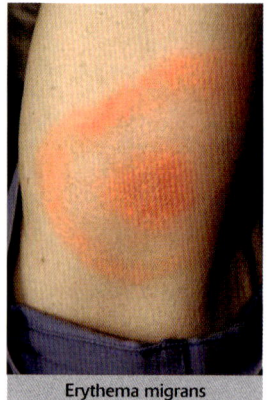

Erythema migrans

Treatment. – Consult a GP if you have symptoms of Lyme disease. Inform the GP the date on which the tick bite occurred and how you removed the tick. As with most infections, Lyme disease is more manageable when diagnosed early, and treatment with a course of antibiotics is usually sufficient.

Risk Reduction. – By taking some simple steps, you can reduce the risk of coming into contact with ticks. Walk on clear, defined paths wherever possible and avoid brushing against vegetation; keep clear of dense vegetation. Wearing light-coloured or unpatterned clothing makes ticks easier to spot and brush off. Carry out regular 'tick checks' both during and at the end of your walk, and once again when you return home. Consider spraying your clothing with an anti-tick pesticide, sold by outdoor shops and chemists. But always follow the instructions carefully.

Removing ticks safely. – The main aim is to remove all parts of the tick's body to prevent it from releasing additional saliva or regurgitating its stomach contents into the bite wound. Use a specialist tick removal tool available from most vets and pet shops. The panel on the right shows two of the most common types of removal tools; the hook and the loop are designed to be twisted to facilitate removal. Both of these devices will grip the head of the tick without squashing the body.

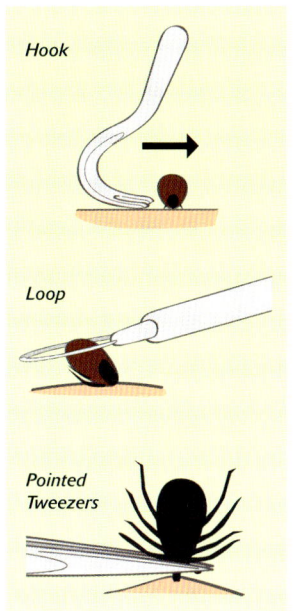

Hook

Loop

Pointed Tweezers

Alternative Methods: With **pointed** tweezers, grasp the tick as close to the skin as possible without squeezing the tick's body, pull the tick out without twisting – there may be considerable resistance. If there are no removal tools available, rather than delay, use a cotton thread. Tie a single loop of cotton around the tick's mouthparts, as close to the skin as possible, then pull gently upwards and outwards.

Do start by cleansing the tweezers with disinfectant. After removing the tick, clean the bite site and the tweezers with antiseptic. **Do** wash your hands thoroughly afterwards. **Do** save the tick in a container in case you develop the symptoms of Lyme disease later and label it with the date and the area where the bite occurred.

Do not squeeze or twist the body of the tick, as this may cause the head and body to separate, leaving the tick's head embedded in your skin. **Do not** attempt to remove a tick with your fingernails. Infection can enter via any breaks in your skin, e.g. around the end of your nails. **Do not** crush the tick's body, as this may cause it to regurgitate its infected stomach contents into the bite wound. **Do not** attempt to burn the tick off, apply petroleum jelly, nail polish or any other chemical, as these methods may also result in regurgitation or saliva release into the wound.

Perform a 'tick check' on any children and dogs in your party. – Children, because of their height, may be more likely to get ticks in the hairline, in or around the ears, whereas, adults most often pick up ticks on the lower body - of course, they 'migrate' higher! Moreover, it makes sense for adults to 'tick check' each other, especially in and around the hairline.

On dogs, ticks often attach themselves in crevices and areas with little to no hair, typically in and around the ears, the areas where the insides of the legs meet the body, between the toes, and within skin folds. Keeping pets out of dense vegetation such as bracken, grasses and woods will help to reduce their exposure to ticks. Performing a 'tick check' on your dogs and other pets after returning from being outside will also help to reduce personal risk. Furthermore, If you feel a bump while petting your dog, don't ignore it! Part the dog's fur to get a closer look.

There are many products used to kill and repel ticks in dogs and pets. These include once-a-month topical products, sprays, powders, dips, shampoos and collars. Removal of these parasites from pets employs the same methods used for humans.

Further help and advice. – These two pages incorporate information from Lyme Disease Action, PO Box 235, Penryn. TR10 8WZ. UK – www.lymediseaseaction.org.uk, which has a range of free literature on the subject; and NHS Direct – https://www.nhs.uk/conditions/lyme-disease. More information on Lyme disease and ticks is available from Public Health England, which runs a tick surveillance scheme – www.gov.uk/guidance/tick-surveillance-scheme.

Bibliography

INFORMATION SOURCES

BOOKS

Barker, Malcolm	*Yorkshire, the North Riding*	1977
Bogg, Edmund	*The Charm of the Hambletons*	1926
Bolton, G. Douglas	*Yorkshire Revealed*	1955
Bonser, K. J.	*The Drovers*	1970
Colbeck, Marice	*Yorkshire Moorlands*	1983
Edwards, William	*The Early History of the North Riding*	1924
Elgee, Frank	*Early Man in North-East Yorkshire*	1930
Falconer, Alan	*Rambler's Riding*	1975
Hall, A.	*On Foot in the North York Moors*	1997
Hayes, Raymond	*Old Roads and Pannierways in North-East Yorkshire*	1988
Lefroy, W.C.	*The Ruined Abbeys of Yorkshire*	1891
Leyland, John	*The Yorkshire Coast*	(edn.) 1892
McDonnell, J. (Editor)	*A History of Helmsley, Rievaulx and District*	1963
Mead, Harry	*Inside the North York Moors*	1978
Mead, Harry	*A Prospect of the North York Moors*	2000
Mee, Arthur	*The Kings England: Yorkshire North Riding*	1945
Morris, R. W.	*Yorkshire through Place Names*	1982
Pevsner, Nikolaus	*Yorkshire: The North Riding*	1966
Pevsner, Nikolaus and Neave, David	*Yorkshire: York and the East Riding*	1995
Robinson, Stephen I.	*Her Master's Walks in the Hambleton Hills*	2003
Robinson, Stephen I.	*Her Master's Walks in the Cleveland Hills*	2016
Rhea, Nicholas	*Portrait of the North York Moors*	1985
Ross, Frederick	*Legendary Yorkshire*	1892
Rushton, John	*The Ryedale Story*	1976
Sale, Richard	*A Guide to the Cleveland Way*	1987
Smith, A. H.	*The Place Names of the East Riding of Yorkshire*	1937
Smith, A. H.	*The Place Names of the North Riding of Yorkshire*	1928
Spence, Joan and Bill	*Romantic Ryedale*	1977
Walker, Colin	*A Walker on the Cleveland Way*	1977
White, Walter	*A Month in Yorkshire*	1858

WEBSITES

Captain Cook Memorial Museum Whitby	www.cookmuseumwhitby.co.uk
Captain Cook Country	www.captaincook.org.uk
English Heritage	www.english-heritage.org.uk
Lyme Disease Action	www.lymediseaseaction.org.uk
National Trails – The Cleveland Way	www.nationaltrail.co.uk/cleveland-way
National Trust	www.nationaltrust.org.uk
NHS Choices – Lyme disease	www.nhs.uk/conditions/lyme-disease
North York Moors Moorland Organisation	www.nymmo.org/importance-sheep-moors
North York Moors National Park	www.northyorkmoors.org.uk
The Moorland Association	www.moorlandassociation.org

Addendum

TEMPORARY DIVERSION AT HAYBURN WYKE

On my last survey in April 2018, a diversion was in operation to the north of Hayburn Wyke due to a coastal landslide. **North Yorkshire County Council issued an order to prohibit all pedestrians from using the Cleveland Way and the England Coast Path between grid reference TA00449874 and TA00969714 for a temporary period of six months between 6th April 2018 to 16th September 2018 for public safety.**

The slippage is substantial and the National Trails Officer for the Cleveland Way has informed me that the diversion may continue for at least a year, possibly longer. Moreover, until the area has fully stabilised this part of the trail will remain closed. The diverted route is fully waymarked, and it allows walkers to enjoy a beautiful length of Hayburn Beck walking in the woods of Hayburn Wyke. The diversion adds about one-third of a mile (600m) to this stretch of the Cleveland Way.

ALWAYS FOLLOW THE DIVERSION SIGNS

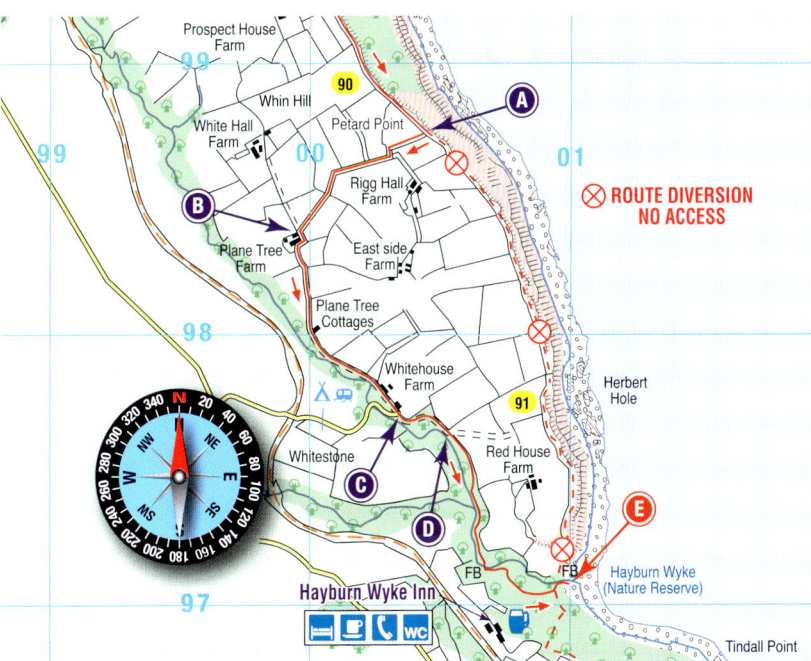

A 004987 Leave the Cleveland Way via a stepstile on the right *(SP Staintondale)*. Follow the left boundary across the field, go through a gate on the left and continue to a farm lane. Turn right and follow the lane to the junction near Plane Tree Farm.

B 999984 Turn left and follow the lane from Plane Tree Farm to Whitehouse Farm and descend to a sharp right bend.

C 003977 Leave the road and follow the narrow lane on the left *(SP Hayburn Wyke)*.

D 005976 Leave the lane via a track on the right and descend to Hayburn Beck. Cross the beck via a footbridge, turn left and follow the track downstream to visit the waterfall at Hayburn Wyke.

E 010971 Route directions continue from **MAP 26 – POINT 19**.

For further updates on this diversion and all other news about the Cleveland Way, please visit the National Trails website www.nationaltrail.co.uk/cleveland-way

Key to the Maps

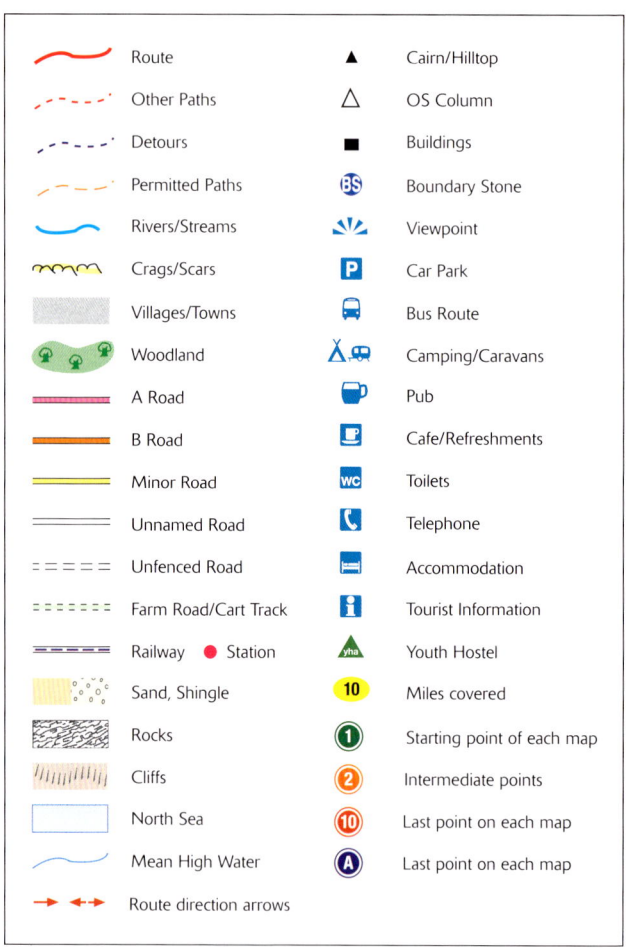